Improving Schools Through Collaborative Enquiry

Improving Schools series
Series editors: Alma Harris and Jane McGregor

How to Improve Your School – Jean Rudduck with Julia Flutter

Leading Teachers – Helen Gunter

Improving Schools in Difficulty – Paul Clarke (Editor)

Improving Schools Through Collaborative Enquiry

Edited by Hilary Street and Julie Temperley

continuum
LONDON • NEW YORK

Continuum International Publishing Group
The Tower Building
11 York Road
London
SE1 7NX

15 East 26th Street
Suite 1703,
New York,
NY 10010, USA

www.continuumbooks.com

© David Jackson, Hilary Street, Julie Temperley, Julie McGrane, Mike Fielding and Sara Bragg 2005

British Library Cataloguing-in-Publication Data
A catalogue record for this book is available from the British Library.

ISBN: 08264 7057 2 (hardback)
        08264 7058 0 (paperback)

Typeset by Fakenham Photosetting Ltd
Printed and bound in Great Britain by Antony Rowe, Chippenham, Wiltshire

'It is frequently the case that practitioners know more than theorists. It is frequently the case that practical knowledge is in advance of theoretical understanding .... Practitioners have a vast corpus of knowledge of pedagogy, of metaphors, of examples of good questions .... The relationship between theoretical and practical knowledge is profound and difficult, with complex interrelations between the two. The biggest challenge will be to cross fertilise those bodies of knowledge.

We know enough about learning. Those principles are well established from experiments, from anthropology, from observation, from class-rooms and from laboratories. But we don't know enough to engineer them in everyday classrooms. The challenge is to finesse this knowledge so that we can hand on something to the next generation of practitioners. It's a major professional challenge to bring it into the classroom.

Practitioners working together collaboratively is an essential process if practitioners in schools are to make sense of this knowledge and understanding so that it can have an impact on classroom practice and therefore on the learning experiences of pupils.'

Professor Charles Desforges at the Networked Learning Communities
Launch Conference, September 2002

Contents

Series Editors' Foreword

This book is written at a time when there is a clear emphasis through both government and non-government departmental bodies on school improvement through collaboration rather than competition and collectivity in preference to individualization. This is evidenced through the promotion of federations, networks and other collegiate arrangements and relationships through a variety of initiatives. In education, as elsewhere, the new century has also been characterized by calls for a greater understanding of the processes of knowledge creation and the transfer of practice. This reflects the increasingly sophisticated practice-based theorizing throughout the social sciences that is developing rapidly and being tested through research.

In identifying and discussing the characteristics of collaborative enquiry and the principles underpinning it, this book crucially moves beyond the rhetoric to acknowledge the complexity of collaboration and knowledge creation in schools and networks of schools. This is explored through the medium of enquiry, which is held to be fundamental to understanding and improving practice in a particular context. An increasing attentiveness to context is also a current theme in educational research, following two decades of centralized changes. Context has been conventionally understood as a container into which generic reforms are dropped, to succeed or fail according to the characteristics of the teachers, parents or children, thereby pathologizing them. Constructivist learning models as employed here present a view of the context of schools and communities as socially constructed over time and linked into wider networks, emphasizing that they are not discrete and enclosed islands, but entities where cultures are continually made and remade by actions and interactions.

The work in this book on enquiry develops the teacher-as-researcher tradition of Lawrence Stenhouse while also extending John Elliot's argument that action–research is distinguished by a transformative aim. The focus is on collaborative enquiry for school improvement, and the audience of those potentially involved moves beyond the orthodox audience of Masters students to encompass a wider constituency of teaching and support staff, governors and students. The central argument is that collaborative enquiry, where it is based on a collectively identified need related to teaching and learning and experience in schools, has greater transformative potential than conventional action enquiry in that it is deliberately designed to influence actions and decisions beyond the group directly involved, thus offering the possibility of system-wide development.

The potentially inclusive dimension of such enquiry is illustrated by the 'three circles model' employed throughout which indicates the importance and equality of value placed on publicly available and validated theory and research, the experiences and tacit knowledge that the actors bring to the work and the new knowledge they subsequently create together; thus offering the possibility of moving across traditional boundaries between academics and teachers, staff and students, good pupils and difficult pupils. The discipline of rigorous enquiry is supported through useful protocols and the empirical examples, which are explored in depth, provide both an absorbing story and a practical insight into collaborative enquiry at different scales.

The authors are teachers, academics and researchers and take the position that collaborative enquiry is a powerful learning methodology where issues identified as important are systematically and collectively investigated and the findings shared for the benefit of others. Such forms of joint work have been consistently identified as most likely to lead to sustained improvement in schools with collaborative working enhancing the capacity to deal with change. Most of the authors are variously linked to the Networked Learning Communities research and development project of the National College of School Leadership which was designed to facilitate collaborative improvement in teaching and learning through enquiry-oriented approaches.

When adults in schools enquire collaboratively, the voice of students inevitably comes to the fore. The chapter on students as researchers extends the concept of collaborative enquiry and builds on the book that launched this series – *How to Improve your School: Giving Pupils a Voice* (Rudduck and Flutter, 2004) to provide an initial typology as a framework for exploring and developing student involvement in enquiry. It draws our attention to the type of relationship and the power relations that operate – from students being involved in enquiry only as a source of data to being co-researchers and as researchers 'in their own right'. Based on research from the Teaching and Learning Research Programme, it provides highly practical suggestions of how to engage with and encourage students as co-researchers in schools and describes Students as Researchers projects, distinguished by the leadership taken by young people. Currently there is considerable interest in pupil participation and consultation, and the caveats offered are timely, for example in reminding us to beware of seeing students as homogeneous and of listening only to those voices which accord with our own dispositions. The transformative potential of relationships forged through such dialogic enquiry and the changing power relations invoked by Helen Gunter (2005) in *Leading Teachers* are evident and overtly championed.

This book tells us that enquiry can be an extroverted activity, engaged with the existing knowledge base of theory and research and also participants' knowledge and understanding of the educational context. By making the familiar unfamiliar, collaborative enquiry can problematize tacit theories and taken-for-granted structures and relationships which shape the (common) experience of school. In acknowledging the possibilities of enquiry we may recognize the openness of the future and the opportunities for change as inviting and energizing.

The book concludes that collaborative enquiry provides a means to make sense of diversity, an active means whereby schools can genuinely develop the capacity to respond appropriately to change and a means whereby leadership as influence can genuinely be distributed and enacted. It brings us new perspectives on school improvement as a process which members of a community can be actively involved with in a practical, challenging but exciting and potentially transformative way. However, it cautions us not to simply see collaboration as an end in itself in relation to enquiry and student voice – but to ask at the start of the process 'Collaboration for what purpose?' It is here that the moral dimension of working on behalf of others to improve teaching and learning and the experience of school comes to the fore, raising questions which call for further exploration around our notions of collaboration, collegiality and community.

JANE MCGREGOR and ALMA HARRIS
Series Editors

References

Gunter, H. (2005) *Leading Teachers*, London: Continuum.
Ruddock, J. and Flutter, J. (2004) *How to Improve your School: Giving Pupils a Voice*, London: Continuum.

Acknowledgements

The authors wish to thank the National College for School Leadership for permission to use the Circles of Knowledge diagram and the Building Capacity diagram. Also to Julie McGrane and Vivienne Baumfield for permission to use the Waves of Involvement diagram.

Glossary

The following terms are used at various times in the book and require a brief explanation as not all readers will be familiar with them.

Best Practice Research Scholarships (BPRS)

Between 2000 and 2003 the DfES in the UK offered 1,000 Best Practice Research Scholarships annually. Their purpose was to enable practitioners to undertake classroom based and sharply focused small-scale studies in priority areas and to apply and disseminate their findings to practitioners elsewhere. The funding was to cover the cost of tutor/mentor support, essential supply cover costs and necessary resources.

Department for Education and Skills (DfES)

This is the UK government department with responsibility for all education and training. It is led by a Secretary of State for Education and a number of Ministers of State, they are elected Members of Parliament. This department is responsible for making education policy.

Economic and Social Research Council (ESRC) Teaching and Learning Research Programme

This programme is part of the work of the Economic and Social Research Council in the UK.

The programme enhances research-based practice in teaching and learning in order to produce significant improvements in outcomes (broadly conceived) for learners. Its remit covers learners of all ages across a wide range of educational and training contexts, including pre-school, primary and secondary school, FE, HE, community, adult and continuing education and the many forms of professional, industrial and commercial learning.

The programme is funded by the HEFCE, DfES, Scottish Executive, National Assembly for Wales and the Northern Ireland Executive and is managed by the ESRC. It fosters partnership between practitioners and researchers in undertaking research and ensuring that it has an impact. Its core objectives are to:

- enhance learning across a range of ages and stages in education, training and lifelong learning;
- develop the capability for transforming the knowledge base relevant to learning into effective and efficient teaching and training practices;
- enhance the UK capacity for research-based practice in teaching and learning;
- promote and extend multidisciplinary and multisector research in teaching and learning.

Education Action Zones (EAZs)

The programme for EAZs began in 1998. EAZs are statutory bodies, funded directly by the Department for Education and Science, but located within Local Education Authorities. They are also expected to raise sponsorship from the private sector. They are located in areas of high social disadvantage and significant educational underachievement. The purpose of EAZs is for groups of schools to work together in partnership with the private sector and local organizations to develop new approaches to raising standards of education in areas of relative deprivation. They come to an end in 2006.

Evidence for Policy and Practice Information and Co-ordinating Centre (EPPI Centre)

The EPPI Centre is part of the Department for Education and Skills initiative to provide evidence to inform policy and practice in education. To support this process the EPPI Centre establishes support groups to conduct systematic reviews of research evidence. It is part of the Social Science Research Unit at the Institute of Education in London.

Foundation Stage, Key Stage One, Two, Three and Four (KS1, KS2, KS3, KS4)

The pupil population in schools in England and Wales is divided into Foundation Stage and four Key Stages. The stages are age related. Foundation Stage includes children age 3 to the end of Reception Year; Key Stage One is pupils in Years 1 and 2, age 5–7; Key Stage Two is pupils in Years 3–6, age 7–11; Key Stage Three is pupils in Years 7–9, age 11–14 and Key Stage Four is pupils in Years 10–11, age 14–16.

General Teaching Council for England (GTCE)

The General Teaching Council for England was established in 1998 by Act of Parliament. It is an independent professional body and has a statutory duty to advise on teaching matters and enable the profession to regulate itself. The principal aims as set out in the 1998 Act are to:

- contribute to improving the standards of teaching and the quality of learning;
- maintain and improve standards of professional conduct amongst teachers.

It finally came into being on 1 September 2000.

Higher Educational Funding Council for England (HEFCE)

The Higher Educational Funding Council for England distributes public money for teaching and research to universities and colleges. In doing so, it aims to promote high-quality education and research within a financially healthy sector. The Council also plays a key role in ensuring accountability and promoting good practice.

In-Service Education and Training (INSET)

The term INSET is used as an abbreviation for In-Service Education and Training. However, the use of this term has decreased in recent years and the term Continuing Professional Development (CPD) is used instead, as it encompasses a wider range of activities than those that might be more narrowly defined as 'training'.

National Education Research Forum (NERF)

The remit of the National Education Research Forum is to oversee the development of a strategy for educational research. It was established by the Secretary of State for Education in 1998 following the recommendations in the report 'Excellence in Research on Schools' by Jim Hillage.

The report called for a 'framework for educational research to place strategic coherence across the current diversity' (Institute of Employment Studies, August 1998, *DfEE Research Brief no. 74*).

National Teacher Research Panel (NTRP)

This is an independent group of practising teachers who work to:

- ensure that all research in education takes account of the teacher perspective;
- ensure a higher profile for research and evidence-informed practice in government;
- increase the number of teachers engaged in and with the full spectrum of research activity.

Office for Standards in Education (Ofsted)

Ofsted is a non-ministerial government department established under the Education (Schools) Act 1992 to take responsibility for the inspection of all schools in England. Its role also includes the inspection of local education authorities, teacher training institutions and youth work. During 2001, Ofsted became responsible for inspecting all 16–19 education and for the regulation of early years' childcare, including childminders.

Specialist Schools Trust (SST)

Founded in 1987 the Specialist Schools Trust is a registered educational charity which acts as the central coordinating body for the specialist schools programme in the UK.

Teacher Training Agency (TTA)

The Teacher Training Agency's purpose is to raise standards in schools by attracting able and committed people to teaching and by improving the quality of practitioner training in England.

In the mid-90s the TTA was able to fund a number of practitioner research projects across the country, known as TTA Research Consortia. It also funded individual practitioners to undertake their own classroom-based research through Practitioner Research Grants.

Introduction

David Jackson and Hilary Street

How 'collaborative enquiry' can help you to study complex professional questions

It is hard for individual practitioners to explore their practice, and the issues and questions it raises about learning and teaching, on their own, which is why the quote from Charles Desforges at the beginning of this book is so important. We need the support of colleagues to make sense of the complexities of our practice. This book is about how we can develop collaborative enquiry amongst practitioners in schools, and between practitioners across schools, and why it is important to do so. It is a book based upon an aspirational view of what teaching as a profession can become, and how a system underpinned by the accumulated knowledge of practitioners can transform learning and teaching.

Imagine an education system designed on a learning paradigm. What might happen if one of the ways in which schools were evaluated was not by predetermined outcomes or by league tables of results, but by the extent to which they contributed their best practice to other schools? Imagine a profession in which practitioners were committed to supporting the learning of children in other schools as well as their own as they learnt more about their craft. Imagine a profession notable for the generosity of creating and giving away professional knowledge for the benefit of others. Such a system would be characterized by professional norms of enquiry and reflection as a foundation for practitioners working and learning from, with and on behalf of others.

A fundamental belief of the authors of this book is that such a system would serve children well and better as professional knowledge accumulated and flowed around the system in ways that have not usually been commonplace in schools.

The world of education is changing. Increasingly, we are moving away from the models of the past (central control, planned change, schools as independent and autonomous units, national strategies) and towards approaches to system development that can make sense of diversity between schools in ways that will contribute to increased learning across the education system and also address issues of social justice. That is the challenge of the twenty-first century for education systems around the world.

Simultaneously, we are entering a networked knowledge era. The dominant discourse is changing from accountability, control, delivery and conformity, towards a discourse about innovation, learning, capacity building, sustainability, interdependence, mutuality and moral purpose based on a belief that these elements are the drivers for learning and growth. Such an education system will be characterized by networks of schools committed to models of shared learning. The process of professional enquiry will underpin professional learning, within and between schools and more widely across the system.

This book advocates informed and disciplined professional enquiry as a foundation for a self-regenerative and self-sustaining learning system. We describe this as 'collaborative enquiry'.

This book has three purposes:

- to demonstrate how practitioners can collaborate to make sense of their professional experience;
- to support practitioners in developing their own understanding of how to undertake the process of enquiry by drawing on the learning from our own experiences;
- to make clear the knowledge base for this work.

The starting point is the school. A school that is supporting collaborative enquiry will have a learning environment and ethos where working practices have been amended and redeveloped so that enquiry is facilitated and encouraged, it is not an isolated activity, and where the school leadership team provides opportunities to enable learning to be shared, discussed by all practitioners and used to inform future practice in the school.

Collaborative enquiry is not an inward-looking activity. One starting point may well be practitioners' own knowledge, understanding and real-life experience. In addition, though, colleagues engaged in collaborative enquiry will establish working practices which mean they actively 'reach out to the knowledge bases', and share responsibility amongst the group to investigate theory as well as research quality practice which already exists and which can provide a foundation for practitioners to take forward their own thinking.

Collaborative enquiry will almost certainly lead to new knowledge being created, both about the focus of the enquiry itself and also about how the process of practitioners enquiring and problem-solving together takes place. Colleagues involved in collaborative enquiry:

- develop a deeper and richer understanding of the particular aspect of learning and teaching being investigated;
- create professional knowledge together that can be transferred within and beyond the school;
- increase the problem-solving capability and adaptive capacity of the school.

Finally we need to say something about our own perspective. The NCSL Networked Learning Communities (NLCs) programme in the UK was beginning its third year of operation (see below).

In April 2001, in response to the publication in the UK of the Department for Education and Skill (DfES) Continuing Professional Development strategy, which had a strong emphasis upon schools as professional learning communities, the newly formed National College for School Leadership (NCSL) submitted a proposal to the DfES. The proposition was that schools seeking to become professional learning communities could achieve this more readily and more profoundly by working together in learning networks. This proposal received government support and backing. The Networked Learning Communities programme was launched in 2002.

At the beginning of 2004 there were 137 Networked Learning Communities in existence, accounting for 1564 schools (6% of all schools) in 93 Local Education Authorities (62% of all LEAs) throughout England.

Three of the authors at the time of writing this book were actively involved in the work of the programme, and the remaining three authors had various connections with aspects of the programme's work. It follows then that the discussion of collaborative enquiry in this book is influenced by our experience of those Networked Learning Communities.

The three fields of knowledge

One of the concepts, or analytical tools, that the programme has developed to underpin its work is that of the 'three fields of knowledge', based on the three fields of knowledge diagram from the NCSL. The circles of knowledge diagram presented on page 4 shows how three different types of knowledge come together in the enquiry process: the craft knowledge of individual practitioners; the knowledge of theory,

Figure 1.1: The three fields of knowledge

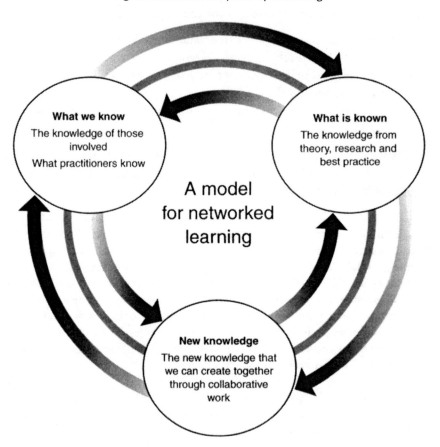

research and practice; and the knowledge created in a community of practitioners engaged in collaborative enquiry.

Often referred to as 'The three fields of knowledge' this model has become common currency amongst Networked Learning Communities participants. It is the template for every programme-learning event and seminar and it is an explicit requirement for all publications to include reference to at least the first two fields and to create opportunities to generate the third. This usually manifests as a tool or resource to support further engagement and learning. The model also articulates a commitment to parity of status for theory and practice and expresses the complex inter-action that takes place between them in professional learning within the programme. Its most compelling message, though, is about the power of collaboration to draw practitioner and public knowledge together to create new understandings, new learning and new knowledge.

What is known ...

This refers to that knowledge which is external, public or validated, and might be national or international research, or the best that is known about practice locally or internationally. But it is essentially both practical and theoretical public knowledge which might serve to frame, support, structure, illuminate or (critically) challenge existing contours of knowledge and training.

What we know ...

This refers to the knowledge which practitioners hold. It includes understandings from their current practice and problems, their context-specific knowledge, their accumulated understanding and insights from prior experience and their enthusiasm for particular dimensions of work, and so on. These are all aspects of practitioner knowledge.

New knowledge ...

This is knowledge which is collaboratively constructed by practitioners or developed through the processes of interaction, design and creation, but built upon what we know and what is known. This third field of knowledge attains its place from a belief that collaborative processes, founded upon respect for existing knowledge, are the vehicle through which innovation and creativity thrive.

We have found this a useful construct for framing our thinking and discussion as it mirrors well the processes that colleagues are developing within the practice of collaborative enquiry.

The Six Levels of Learning

Each NLC has its own learning focus but all have committed themselves to supporting some common principles and ways of working. These include the design framework which comprises six interdependent levels of learning. They are:

1 **Pupil learning**
   NLCs are expected to have a clear pedagogic focus at the heart of their activity.

2 **Adult learning**
   The programme is about creating school cultures where practitioners learn with and alongside their students.

3 **Leadership for learning and leadership development**
   The programme seeks to invest in the capacity of head practitioners,

network leaders and other schools to create the enabling and facilitative conditions for network learning. The programme assumes there is a much wider pool of latent leadership talent than the system currently harnesses. The programme seeks to offer opportunities for that to be developed.

4 Schoolwide learning
The programme is designed to support the development of schools as professional learning communities and to assist also with the internal redesign processes that can support this aspiration.

5 School-to-school learning
This is based on the belief that the best way to encourage practitioners to share knowledge within a school is also to encourage them to share knowledge with others outside the school.

6 Network-to-network learning
A key premise of the NLC programme is that whilst networks help the schools within them to develop local context-specific solutions to the problems they face, schools in other networks should also be able to understand and interpret these solutions and transpose them into their own contexts. In this way network-based organizations are seen to carry the potential to accelerate knowledge creation and innovation right across the education system.

The practitioners in these networks have committed to working collaboratively, to working smarter (learning more powerfully) and to working interdependently (as communities) rather than working harder alone. A part of that commitment is to problem-solve together the adoption of the collaborative enquiry and knowledge sharing processes advocated here.

Questions to the reader

We have included questions to the reader at the end of each section in each chapter. We hope that readers will find this helpful in engaging more actively with the discussion presented. We also felt that it was important to model 'The three circles of knowledge' diagram and invite colleagues to construct the knowledge and thinking with us.

A note about language

Clarity of terms

Much of the writing about collaborative enquiry is new and has had a variety of antecedents. This results on occasion in a possible confusion and lack of clarity in the language with different vocabulary being used to describe similar processes. For example, the development of activities that fall under the umbrella of collaborative enquiry, professional enquiry, communities of enquiry and professional learning communities have had a varied and disparate development.

Consequently the relevant literature does not use the language consistently. In this book we are using the terms 'collaborative enquiry' and 'professional enquiry' to refer to similar activities. 'Communities of enquiry' as we have stated are both an outcome of the enquiry process and also a description of the process of collaborative enquiry itself – hence it is a doubly powerful concept.

Two other concepts are also developed in much of the literature about professional learning and enquiry: the notion of a 'learning community' and a 'professional learning community', again we see these terms as describing the same concept. The concept of a professional learning community is important for an understanding of collaborative enquiry and we discuss this further in Chapter 2. Collaborative enquiry has an important contribution to make to the development of professional learning communities. It is the change to a professional learning community that brings about transformation in an organization.

Practitioners

Throughout the text we have used the term 'practitioners' to denote the adults participating in collaborative enquiry. The term is intended to include the full range of professionals who might participate in school. Thus teachers, headteachers, others with leadership responsibility, school librarians, technicians and classroom or learning support assistants might all be indicated by the use of the term 'practitioner'. Where it is important or more helpful, for instance in relation to a particular role in collaborative enquiry or in an account of practice to be more specific, the actual designation (teacher, headteacher, etc.) is used. In many cases collaborative enquiry includes the full participation of pupils. As the involvement of young people is dealt with extensively in Chapter 4, we have not attempted to deal with pupil participation elsewhere, believing that the complementarity and connections between practitioner and pupil models for collaborative enquiry speak for themselves.

Students or pupils?

Deciding whether to use the word student or pupil to describe the young people in our schools was difficult as use does vary with the age of the young person and the context. In the end we decided to use whichever word was most appropriate in the context in which we were writing. In Chapter 4 we have used the word 'student' all the way through even though some of the examples are of primary children, because the concept Students as Researchers now exists as a construct regardless of phase of school.

1   Collaborative enquiry: why bother?

David Jackson and Hilary Street

> Without passion life and routine are sterile; with passion they are exciting
> and meaningful, and knowledge is not simply accumulated but also trans-
> formed.
>
> (Mitchell and Sackney, 2000, p. 44)

Collaborative enquiry as a 'way of being' in schools has the potential
to transform the way practitioners think about and relate to the core
business of learning and teaching, and in that sense is able to support the
transformation of schools.

This chapter seeks to answer the following questions:

1 What is collaborative enquiry?
2 Why is collaborative enquiry an important concept at this time?

A brief summary of the main issues to be discussed is given at the
beginning of each section.

1. What is collaborative enquiry?

The remainder of this book expands in detail what exactly 'collaborative
enquiry' is and what it looks like in practice. The following is simply a
brief overview of the concept. In this section there is a discussion of:

- the development of collaborative enquiry and a definition of the
  concept;
- a discussion of the distinctive nature of collaborative enquiry;
- collaborative enquiry as a form of research.

The development of collaborative enquiry

The massive increase during the 1990s of 'applied research components'
in masters degrees and the rise of the school effectiveness and school
improvement movements were key levers in encouraging a shift of focus
and emphasis within schools towards a culture that was more likely to
encourage practitioner research into their own practice. This, coupled

with the increased discontent about 'traditional' educational research and (with a few notable exceptions) its lack of impact on practice, gave new impetus to school-based research. This was supported strategically at a national level by developments such as the TTA Research Scholarships, the Best Practice Research Scholarships and the TTA School-Based Research Consortia.

In addition, more recently the work of the National Education Research Forum (NERF) and the National Teacher Research Panel (NTRP) have also given extra focus to the development of research that involves practitioners in partnership with the research community and is relevant to practitioners' perceived needs. Further support for the process of linking more closely and effectively research and classroom practice has come from the national ESRC Teaching and Learning Research Programme which has one strand looking at 'Research Capacity – building networks'. The work of the EPPI Centre quoted later in this book is another strategy for bridging the gap between practice and research by undertaking systematic research reviews on specific topics that will have relevance for practitioners.

Practitioners' research has therefore developed as an important part of formal CPD. Where it was effective it often had positive outcomes for the individual practitioners involved and enhanced their own learning and practice. Although there were often systems in place for disseminating written reports of the work there was often no way of working that was integral to the research process itself which involved individual practitioners collaborating with others.

Systematic enquiry is enhanced and encouraged if there is a requirement and expectation on the part of the practitioners involved that they will be required to make their findings public.

Towards a definition

Collaborative enquiry is a particular example of school-based research. It is a much broader activity than most previous school-based research, which was usually undertaken as an individual activity. Collaborative enquiry is for a more general purpose. It involves individual practitioners in a school choosing to come together to investigate and learn more about an aspect of their practice in order to enhance the learning of the children they teach or the school as an educational community. They do this by engaging with current theory and research, gathering information about that aspect of their practice under investigation, analysing and reflecting together on the information gathered and identifying how practice needs to develop in the light of their investigations.

In doing so they are able to design better and more effective interventions and strategies for use in their own classrooms and their school, which can be shared with other colleagues in the school (or network). Maurice Galton (2002) refers to this as a 'replicable process' rather than 'generalisable findings'. It is more public, more shared and more likely to contribute to the wider knowledge base of learning and teaching than some of the previous examples listed and more likely to contribute to the learning of others.

By working in this way they are creating new knowledge (their learning) and adding to the knowledge base for a wider group of professionals. That sense of doing it for the benefit of children, their own learning and the learning of others is a powerful motivator – practitioners contributing to the progressively expanding knowledge base of the profession on behalf of, and increasingly with, children. Pupils have a role to play in this process, too, and Chapter 4 in this book explores the significant and distinctive role of pupils in enquiry in more detail. This explicit commitment to publicizing and sharing the new knowledge is a key component of collaborative enquiry. But it is important to note that the sharing is taking place not because there is an assumption of a straightforward 'transfer' between schools or classes, but because there is an assumption that this new knowledge can be adapted and redesigned by colleagues in other contexts. It is about transfer of best process rather than for best practice (Galton 2002).

The distinctive nature of collaborative enquiry

It is this notion of an activity beyond the group of colleagues who are specifically engaged in the enquiry process that distinguishes enquiry, as we are describing it, from some other forms of action research. What gives collaborative enquiry its distinctive 'flavour' and 'potency' is the fact that it is specifically designed to involve a group of colleagues investigating together, and is intended to move beyond the actual colleagues undertaking the enquiry to involve the wider school community both within and across schools. It is designed to contribute to the collective professional knowledge pool and to influence broadly as well as specifically, the classrooms of the core participants. In environments in which change is happening fast – and that is certainly true of schools – it is a means by which a number of groups of staff can learn 'on behalf of' the wider school and educational community.

This takes place within the context of their own school, but increasingly, as school-to-school networks become more prevalent, they may also be doing it within the context of collaboration with practitioners in other schools. Finally, as the Networked Learning Communities programme has shown, there will increasingly be network-to-network learning.

Collaborative enquiry as a form of research

The use of the word 'research' has proved problematic for some practitioners – in both the school and the research communities. For some colleagues in schools the word continues to carry with it restrictive connotations and conventions of 'academic research' far removed from the day-to-day needs, demands and pressures of school life. Conversely, for 'academic' colleagues 'school-based research' is often perceived as lacking the rigour and 'purity' of academic research.

Adopting the term 'collaborative enquiry' is an attempt to break out of this bind. It is a means of defining new conventions and protocols. This means generating research designs that are valid and reliable in relation to their purpose and their school context, rather than focusing on the design or the abstract purity or validity of the knowledge or the extent to which it can be generalized. In one of the examples used later in the book practitioners knew that they wanted to teach Thinking Skills more effectively. The strategies that they and the pupils used to research what exactly was going on when they were teaching and learning about Thinking Skills included the use of video, practitioner and pupil logs, focused group discussion and residentials. In another example, a primary school's focus of enquiry was to address the transition from Foundation Stage to Year One for pupils, to make it less traumatic in terms of the sudden shift from learning through play, and at Key Stage Two they wanted to enquire further into the reasons for the underachievement of boys in literacy. The enquiry strategies used by the school included a number of actual training sessions where they considered and used the existing research knowledge on their two areas of enquiry; analysed and discussed this information with colleagues and then applied it to their own context. These strategies met their enquiry needs and produced information that was itself immediately useful to the staff concerned as well as potentially valuable to practitioners elsewhere within their network of schools. Perhaps most importantly of all, the strategies made sense to the practitioners involved and were doable.

Technically simple but socially complex

School-based collaborative enquiry has been described as being technically simple but socially complex. The important point to note is that whilst collaborative enquiry may be technically more straightforward than traditional research, that does not mean it is simplistic or without its own rigour. Indeed the very fact of collaborating with colleagues brings with it a pressure for rigour as part of the process of accountability to fellow practitioners. It tends to be easier for one practitioner working alone to engage in more idiosyncratic and esoteric activity than when it is a group of practitioners working together. Collaboration brings discipline to the enquiry process itself. As part of its own 'scaffolding' to support the process of enquiry the NLC programme has used the criteria developed by the National Teacher Research Panel as its yardstick to ensure rigour in the research processes being used. (They are included at the end of this chapter.)

Collaborative enquiry is 'socially complex' because it requires practitioners both to work together in depth to research, question, discuss and reflect on their own practice, and at the same time investigate the knowledge that already exists about their chosen focus as well as work together to make sense of their own knowledge and external knowledge and research. Effectively it is a group of peers facilitating learning for each other, and being honest with each other about their own practice and beliefs. This requires a high level of intra and interpersonal skills, including skills of facilitation, an understanding of group processes and effective communication, as well as personal qualities including honesty, sensitivity, commitment and trust.

> To what extent do colleagues in your school or organization already use research evidence to inform their practice?
>
> What opportunities exist for colleagues to work together easily on specific aspects of practice?

2. Why is collaborative enquiry an important concept at this time?

Collaborative enquiry is an essential professional activity for any school community that wishes to continue to grow and develop. It is axiomatic that staff in schools will wish to continue their professional journey for as long as they have children to teach, regardless of any external political imperatives. However, the current external context within which schools in the UK and elsewhere are operating makes collaborative enquiry as a way of working even more important. In this section we aim to:

- describe the political context within which collaborative enquiry is currently taking place by discussing briefly the concept of 'informed

professionalism' and the shift away from 'top-down' government
initiatives;
• setting collaborative enquiry within a framework of school
improvement;
• make the link with the transformation agenda and cultural change
leadership and sustainability;
• show how collaborative enquiry supports capacity building in an
organization.

**The political context for collaborative enquiry, the move towards
'informed professionalism' and the shift from 'top-down' government
initiatives**

The political context and agenda for education in 2003 shifted consid-
erably in favour of more autonomy and trust in the teaching profession as
a whole. Michael Barber, whilst head of the government's Standards and
Effectiveness Unit in the UK, offered the following schematic analysis of
the shift in context over the last four decades.

Figure 1.1: The quadrant diagram

1980s Uninformed prescription	1970s Uninformed professionalism
1990s Informed prescription	2000s Informed professionalism

Michael Barber (while Head of the DfES Standards and Effectiveness Unit)

Although clearly there is discussion about the model, the concept of
informed professionalism in the twenty-first century is not in dispute.
Definitions of professionalism vary but we have chosen to use that
offered by the General Teaching Council for England (GTCE). They
define professionalism as being about trust, accountability and authority,
and describe the elements of professionalism in the following way:

Common dimensions of professionalism can be expressed like this:

• *Professionals act altruistically and ethically in the interests of their
clients, drawing on their specialist knowledge and skill.*
The GTC has been at pains to re-emphasize the moral and social basis
of teaching in the context of a political discourse that has seemed to
emphasize delivery and performance.

- *Professionals maintain and regulate transparent standards and do so in the public interest.*
  Council Members have drafted and consulted on a Code of Professional Practice, and also ensured that its principles are enshrined in the standards for QTS.

- *Professionals lead the ideas within their field.*
  The GTC takes seriously the idea of 'distributed' leadership. Responsibility for educational leadership – by which we mean leading learning – is not restricted to senior management teams in schools but is rather about practitioners having the competence, confidence, status and support to lead the pedagogical and curriculum development ideas in their field.

(Lesley Saunders, GTCE, 2002)

The phrase 'informed professionalism' is highly relevant in the context of 'collaborative enquiry'. Professionals do not suddenly 'become informed' by some process of osmosis. Systems, working practices and opportunities have to be put in place to enable them to be 'informed'. We see 'informed professionalism' as a concept which has at its core a belief amongst practitioners in the importance of their practice being characterized by ongoing reflection about learning and teaching. This requires active engagement with investigation about the learning processes in their own classrooms and school, and a knowledge of and engagement with relevant research and practice. There is an implicit assumption that informed professionalism requires practitioners to work together and share and support each other's learning. Such professional growth is much less likely to happen in isolation from other practitioners. It is this that makes collaborative enquiry such an important tool to support the growth of 'informed professionalism'.

Given this shift in emphasis to 'informed professionalism' as well as the development of a more distributed approach to leadership in schools, then the development of schools receptive to and facilitative of collaborative enquiry is an important, purposeful and powerful strategy for leaders in schools to develop with their staff.

The current political agenda for education

In 2003, the UK government's policy agenda for education made it clear that they recognized that the 'top-down' centrally imposed change agenda of the previous ten years was not sustainable in the long term, not least because it was not sufficiently motivating for staff and ran the risk of stifling professional creativity.

For schools to continue to improve the educational achievement of all pupils, practitioners will have to be given greater freedom and autonomy to find their own solutions and ways forward in response to future challenges. For example, Lorna Earl (2003) and her team, in their evaluation of the national literacy and numeracy strategies in the UK, are clear that the strategies have run their course and are unlikely to continue to make the same degree of impact in the future.

A number of writers and researchers have commented in recent years on the limitations of large-scale 'top-down' reform initiatives. David Hopkins (who was Head of the Standards and Effectiveness Unit at the DfES) noted that

> More of the same will not produce sustained results. Informed prescription is a way to start national initiatives, but it will not give sustained improvement. ... There is a ground swell of support for greater collaborative working across schools. The government is developing policies to support that.
>
> (Hopkins 2003)

This theme was also developed by David Hargreaves (2003) who observes, when discussing the implications of the 'transformation' agenda, that

> a second driver is the growing recognition that the improvement strategies hitherto adopted have inevitable limitations. Between 1997 and 2002, the literacy and numeracy strategies in primary schools were among the most impressive of the government's achievement in Education. But the rate of improvement has levelled off. The literacy and numeracy strategies were a new top-down, highly prescriptive lever, which despite much early opposition to this undoubted challenge to the professional autonomy of primary school teachers has on the whole worked. ... All levers have their limits. Educational processes are complex, affected by many variables, so the amount of improvement any single lever can effect is smaller than reformers might wish.
>
> (p. 21)

Schools have to be able to 'transform' themselves to meet the challenges of the twenty-first century and become 'professional learning communities'. More importantly, they also need to be able to learn from one another, so that professional gains accumulate. To do this Hopkins believes that:

- schools need to build in time for collective enquiry because such collective enquiry creates the structural conditions for school improvement;
- studying classroom practice increases the focus on student learning;
- the process of engaging in collective enquiry involves using the research on teaching and learning in order to take forward school improvement efforts;

- by working in small groups the whole school staff can become a 'nurturing unit';
- professional development as enquiry provides synergy and enhanced student effects.

Cooperation not competition

By 2003 in the UK there was a significant change in government policy towards education with an explicit emphasis on cooperation between schools rather than competition, and on the need for schools to learn from each other in a context where all have something to contribute. This emphasis on collaboration and cooperation between schools in contrast to the competition of the previous ten years is welcome, but it is also extremely hard to achieve in practice – it is itself a learning challenge. Schools are busy places, practitioners have no 'spare' time in the school day and there are often insufficient enabling structures in place to make such cooperation and collaboration happen easily. Schools, as we have noted earlier, even find it hard to disseminate and share good practice within their own organizational boundaries. The irony, though, is that it is often easier (though still difficult) for practitioners to share their good practice with colleagues outside their own school than with those in their own school.

The changing nature of Continuing Professional Development (CPD)

The crucial role of ongoing Continuing Professional Development is now generally recognized and agreed. In 2003 in England the first DfES/NCSL online event for CPD took place, enabling practitioners to go online and engage with policy-makers to share their views on the subject. The GTCE advocates a model of professional learning in their publication *The Practitioners' Professional Learning Framework*. Finally, where the Performance Management Review (PMR) process is working effectively in schools, then CPD is an integral and effective part of PMR. The Innovation Unit at the DfES is piloting 'innovation exchange' methodologies and the Networked Learning Communities programme and the Specialist Schools Trust are each holding regular formal events focused upon the sharing of knowledge between both schools and networks of schools. This changing approach to CPD, with an emphasis on teaching as a research-informed profession and a move towards more collaborative arrangements between schools and to knowledge sharing across the system, requires the development of collaborative enquiry.

At this point it may be helpful to clarify exactly what is meant by teaching as a research-informed profession and the use of, engagement with and engagement in research by practitioners, as it is an area that has proved complex and challenging.

Teaching as a research-informed profession

Ongoing professional development and learning is essential for continued professional growth. It includes keeping abreast of relevant research and being clear about the implications of that research for one's own practice, although, as we discuss elsewhere in this chapter, practitioners' access to and engagement with educational research has been deeply problematic in the past. Issues of relevance, access and usability are some of the key barriers to effective use. In recent years the UK has seen a sea-change in the way in which educational research is being undertaken and the way in which the practitioner and research communities are beginning to relate to each other. This change has resulted in more collaborative work between practitioners and HE colleagues, more school-based research and enquiry and more thought given to the ways in which research can be made accessible, shared and used. This has led to a significant growth in the number of practitioners who now regularly 'engage' with research, and a growth too in the number of practitioners who are undertaking research themselves in their classrooms and their schools.

However, there is a need to clarify some of the language used when discussing teaching as a 'research-informed' profession. At its most straightforward this phrase is commonly used to describe how practitioners can use and relate to current research about teaching and learning in order to continue to develop and enhance their practice. The literature talks variously about 'research-informed practice', 'engaging with research' and 'engaging in research'. For the purposes of this book we find 'research-informed practice' a useful starting point when discussing collaborative enquiry.

The examples of collaborative enquiry described in this book show groups of practitioners working together in such a way that their learning and teaching are research informed. An integral part of the enquiry process is to investigate (enquire into) what research and knowledge already existed about the particular focus of the enquiry. The examples involve practitioners working with a HE partner, part of whose responsibility was to seek out and share relevant research with them, and to help the practitioners to 'work' with the research and think through the implications of it for their practice. This is an example of research-informed practice. For research-informed practice to take place, ways of working need to be developed and processes need to be in place that enable practitioners to have easy access to relevant and timely research.

The important point to note is that it is not sufficient to simply have the 'research evidence', it must be embedded in some sort of learning process if practitioners are to be able to use it effectively. Cordingley (2003) notes that 'the use of research or research and evidence-informed practice needs, therefore, to be understood as at least as complex and technically demanding an activity as conducting the research in the first place' (p. 108).

Joyce and Showers (1988) noted in their research about the link between knowledge of research and impact on practice that there was very little impact on practice because practitioners had no real personal control or mastery of the research until they had had the opportunity to:

- absorb information and theory*;
- see theory demonstrated;
- practise putting theory to work in classrooms;
- receive feedback based on observation of their practice, together with expert coaching on a sustained basis.

(*and we would add 'and work and reflect on it with colleagues')

Engaging in research

Many of the practitioners in the examples in this book were also engaged in an enquiry process in their own classrooms, as an integral part of collaborative enquiry. Increasingly, research is the result of a partnership or 'joint venture' between practitioners and research colleagues in HE. As Lesley Saunders (2002) notes, this leads to a much wider view of what the evidence base is for a research and evidence-based profession.

> Some of the most valuable research is coming from teacher-led, school-based research, supported by scholarly expertise and methodological protocols provided by academics. So we need to understand the 'evidence base' for teaching, not as a body of finite, prescribable knowledge, but rather as a living process built around and tested on practical experience in the classrooms, developed from and adapted to particular teaching and learning settings.
>
> (p. 6)

She notes also that teachers engaging with and in research would be helped to:

- *reflect* on their practice;
- *reclaim* the language and discourse of pedagogy;
- *relate* professionally with their colleagues in schools and universities, and collaborate on experiments in teaching and learning;

- *reinforce* the need for an evidence-driven approach to innovation;
- *restore* a sense of exploration, invention and creativity to classroom planning and practice;
- create a more naturally paced, naturally-scaled *reform* – school-led school improvement, even?

The GTC(E) is working on some core principles for research-informed practice and believes that 'research-informed professional practice' helps teachers to:

- make beliefs and tacit knowledge explicit, and reflect collectively on pedagogy, assessment, the curriculum and school leadership;
- scrutinise, compare and appraise underpinning theories;
- unpick simplistic notions of cause and effect, and develop more forensic and situated models (for example, about factors affecting pupil learning and performance);
- develop new ideas and concepts from a foundation of existing good practice and theory;
- create, interpret, share and rigorously evaluate practical evidence about teaching and learning in and for different contexts;
- be engaged individually and collectively in the spectrum of research/ enquiry, from individual classroom-based action research projects to large-scale 'academic' studies;
- create 'sound' professional knowledge for educational decision-making.

(GTC(E) 2004)

The feedback from those teachers who are engaging with research, and in many cases undertaking enquiries into their own practice, is that they find this a professionally energizing and positive experience, and not something that is an additional burden. Usually this is because where such activity is occurring, the school has organized ways of working that enable this to be integrated with normal daily practice and routines, and made opportunities within school time for the activities to take place. But the process does have to be managed effectively. Collaborative enquiry is an approach which enables practitioners to engage both in and with research in a way that fits with their normal daily practice.

The difference between enquiry and research

Not all teacher enquiries will be designed to be shared widely in a public form, even though they may well be shared amongst close peers with whom practitioners are working. Teachers enquiring into their classrooms is an important professional learning experience and opportunity but it is not 'research'. However it does mean that the practice is 'evidence' based – because the practitioners have been explicitly seeking evidence about aspects of their classrooms and practice. Cordingley (2003) explores this conundrum at length and observes that 'Whether or not it is research-informed practice depends upon whether the teacher involved drew upon the research of others' (p. 108).

What does come through in much of the literature about practitioner use of research is that for it to be used effectively the practitioners themselves, whilst not having to engage in 'full-blown' research, are better able to make sense of and work with others' research if they are engaged in some sort of enquiry process themselves. This then gives a 'live' context to which they can relate the research of others.

For practitioners to be described as engaging in research themselves then a range of research protocols would need to be followed and would inform the design of the process. Earlier we cited the criteria used by the NTRP and they are included at the end of this chapter. They provide a useful framework for teacher-led research.

Lesley Saunders encapsulates the difference when quoting from the work of Hiebert *et al.* (2002), though she notes that of course the distinction is not completely unproblematic.

Practitioner knowledge is they say
• linked with practice and problems of practice
• detailed, concrete and specific
• integrated rather than differentiated

Professional knowledge on the other hand is
• public and examinable
• storable and sharable
• verifiable and capable of improvement

(Saunders 2002, p. 6)

School improvement: a framework for collaborative enquiry
The dimensions of the wider political context and the development of informed professionalism described above, though important, are not a sufficient rationale for collaborative enquiry. It is the link with school-improvement processes which is crucial to an understanding of why collaborative enquiry is such an important concept.

School improvement and the transformation agenda are about change, but that change must be managed in such a way that it not only achieves its intended outcomes but also strengthens the capacity of staff in the school to deal with the challenges they will continue to face in the context of the developing 'knowledge society'.

The key elements in the research and knowledge base about school improvement which provide the context and the incentive for collaborative enquiry are discussed below. They include:

- *the move towards 'authentic school improvement'*
  A shift from national initiatives to a 'third stage' of school improvement which David Hopkins describes as 'authentic school improvement';

- *the implications of the knowledge society*
  An emphasis on the development of a school culture that is able to respond to the complex and rapidly changing context in which schools work, particularly given the implications of the knowledge society (see p. 26);

- *facilitative conditions for learning and teaching*
  The importance of focusing on learning and teaching and at the same time ensuring that the organizational conditions support this focus on learning and teaching;

- *the development of learning-centred leadership*
  The development of learning-centred leadership and, as part of that, the development of distributed leadership in schools;

- *learning-enriched schools*
  The importance of developing 'learning-enriched' schools where continuing professional development is planned and designed to enhance both pupil and practitioner learning.

They are discussed separately below.

The move towards 'authentic school improvement'
David Hopkins (2001) describes the shift from national initiatives as a move to a 'third stage' of 'authentic school improvement'. School improvement is at an important point in its development. It is clear that the current approach to the reform agenda is not sufficient to enable schools, whatever their stage of development, to continue to improve and develop, and more importantly not even sufficient to help them sustain their current achievements or give them the capacity to deal with the challenges facing education in the twenty-first century.

Hopkins, amongst others, notes that the government's approach to the reform agenda with its emphasis on nationally generated and designed programmes, although useful at helping schools move from a moderately low to an average level of achievement, are often only short term in their effects, and reach a plateau. Nor are they sufficient for the majority of schools who need to sustain their development in the long term. The thrust of Hopkins' argument is that externally generated change does not impact sufficiently on the classroom.

The first stage of school improvement was characterized by an emphasis on individual strategies in individual schools. They were 'too fragmented in their conception and application and therefore struggled to impact on classroom practice' (Hopkins 2001, p. 53).

The second stage of school improvement provided more tools, and was built on a merger of research on school improvement and school effectiveness. Some of the developments that characterized the second stage of school improvement were added guidelines, strategies for implementation of improvement strategies that were sufficiently powerful to affect classrooms and a more coherent approach to staff development and development planning. 'It is clear that neither the first nor second stage of school improvement has made sufficient impact at the learning level' (ibid., p. 54).

Hopkins sets out his own framework for the third stage which he describes as 'authentic school improvement', which he believes is more likely to have an impact on the learning of both staff and pupils. Collaborative enquiry is a central part of that framework. The principles of authentic school improvement are set out below.

In general, 'authentic' school improvement programmes are:

- *Achievement focused* – they focus on enhancing student learning and achievement, in a broader sense than mere examination results or test scores.
- *Empowering in aspiration* – they intend to provide those involved in the change process with the skills of learning and 'change agentry' that will raise levels of expectation and confidence throughout the educational community.
- *Research based and theory rich* – they base their strategies on programmes and programme elements that have an established track record of effectiveness, that research their own effectiveness and connect to and build on other bodies of knowledge and disciplines.
- *Context specific* – they pay attention to the unique features of the school situation and build strategies on the basis of an analysis of that particular context.

- *Capacity building in nature* – they aim to build the organisational conditions that support continuous improvement.
- *Enquiry driven* – they appreciate that reflection-in-action is an integral and self-sustaining process.
- *Implementation oriented* – they take a direct focus on the quality of classroom practice and student learning.
- *Interventionist and strategic* – they are purposely designed to improve the current situation in the school or system and take a medium-term view of the management of change, of planning and prioritise developments accordingly.
- *Externally supported* – they build agencies around the school that provide focused support, and create and facilitate networks that disseminate and sustain 'good practice'.
- *Systematic* – they accept the reality of centralised policy context, but also realise the need to adapt external changes for internal purpose, and to exploit the creativity and synergies existing within the system.

(ibid., pp. 16–17)

Collaborative enquiry with its emphasis on practitioner and pupil learning is an important element of this third stage, and a key part of authentic school improvement. The link between the elements of the framework and collaborative enquiry are shown in the table below.

Achievement focused	The purpose of engaging in collaborative enquiry is to enhance the learning of both practitioners and pupils. By practitioners developing their own knowledge and understanding, and linking that with their own classroom processes, learning is enhanced.
Empowering in aspiration	Practitioners choose to engage in collaborative enquiry, and it is they themselves who identify the focus and decide which processes they will use. They have considerable autonomy and the processes they engage in will develop a range of other skills as well as developing their own knowledge. Such experiences are life-enhancing and empowering. The quotes from practitioners in this book demonstrate this.
Research based and theory rich	An essential part of collaborative enquiry involves reading about and working with the knowledge and research base that already exists. Most collaborative enquiries involve the practitioners working with an external partner, often from HE, who supports the identification and use of relevant research and works with practitioners to ensure working practices that help the theory from the practice be explored.

Context specific	Collaborative enquiries are 'site-based' initially, and derive from practitioners current practice and context. The learning developed takes place in that context, and even if practitioners are working in a wider network the fixed point of reference is always their own context.
Capacity building in nature	The process of collaborative enquiry builds individual practitioner capacity in terms of their knowledge and the skills they develop. It also contributes to developing capacity across the organization because groups of practitioners are involved so the collective capacity of staff is enhanced. Moreover, the organization itself develops its own working practices that enable the development of a learning community which enhances the capacity of all members to develop and grow.
Enquiry driven	By definition collaborative enquiry requires practitioners to investigate aspects of practice and to reflect on and analyse them. This becomes the 'taken-for-granted' way of working.
Implementation oriented, and interventionist and strategic	One of the purposes of collaborative enquiry is to change and amend practice and therefore to make interventions. It is a strategic process too because it is a way of working that is focused, planned, formally led, has a time-line, is integrated with the work of the school and is expected to impact on practice. It can also be developed across the whole school.
Externally supported	Most collaborative enquiry groups have some sort of external support and facilitation. This may be a HE colleague and/or a member of staff in school who acts as coordinator for the enquiry process and who is the link with HE. Such support is essential to provide an ongoing structure and momentum and in the context of the HE link, a conduit for research.
Systematic	All collaborative enquiry takes place 'in context' and this refers to both the internal and external context. Collaborative enquiry is systematic because it: • creates a 'hunger' for data which is gathered in a planned way and used creatively and collaboratively; • means careful choices are made about the strategies that are most 'fit for the purpose' of gathering the data; • ensures reflection and analysis of the data are built into the working processes and subsequent action agreed to ensure impact; • makes sure explicit processes for sharing and disseminating the learning are identified and implemented.

The implications of the knowledge society

This requires an emphasis on the development of a school culture that is able to respond to the complex and rapidly changing context in which schools work, and encourage sustainability, particularly given the implications of the knowledge society.

In the introduction to his book about teaching in the knowledge society Andy Hargreaves (2003) defines the knowledge society in the following way:

> We live in a knowledge economy, a knowledge society. Knowledge economies are stimulated and driven by creativity and ingenuity. Knowledge society schools have to create these qualities, otherwise their people and their nations will be left behind ... the knowledge society is, in Joseph Schumpeter's terms, a force of creative destruction. It stimulates growth and prosperity but its relentless pursuit of profit and self-interest also strains and fragments the social order. ... The term knowledge society is actually a misnomer. I stick with it in this book because of its widespread and accepted usage ... a knowledge society is really a learning society. ... Knowledge societies process information and knowledge in ways that maximise learning, stimulate ingenuity and invention and develop the capacity to initiate and cope with change.
>
> (p. xvi)

He goes on to summarize how organizations in a knowledge society have to develop a range of capacities amongst their staff by raising skill levels and retraining, breaking down barriers to learning, getting people to work in overlapping teams and networks, seeing mistakes as opportunities for learning, involving everyone in the 'big picture', developing 'social capital' and ensuring that everyone has the support they need for further learning. These developments are as essential for schools as for any other organization and developing collaborative enquiry as one of the ways of working is a strategy for achieving much of this. He sets out what this means for practitioners in schools:

> What might it mean in practical terms for practitioners to be catalysts of the knowledge society, to be the key agents who can bring it into being? How would this mandate affect their role, as well as their own and other people's understandings of what being a professional entails?
>
> In general, as catalysts of successful knowledge societies, practitioners must be able to build a special kind of professionalism. This cannot be the professionalism of old, where practitioners had the autonomy to teach in the ways they wished, or that were most familiar to them. There is no value in reviving the Julie Andrews curriculum – 'these are few of my favourite things' – where practitioners could teach anything they liked. Rather, practitioners must build a new professionalism, the main components of which are outlined below.
>
> (*ibid.*, pp. 15–16)

He goes on to describe practitioners as catalysts of the knowledge society, and identifies the following actions which they will need to take:

- promote deep cognitive learning;
- learn to teach in ways they were not taught;
- commit to continuous professional learning;
- work and learn in collegial teams;
- treat parents as partners in learning;
- develop and draw on collective intelligence;
- build a capacity for change and risk;
- foster trust in process.

Collaborative enquiry as part of a school-improvement change process fits well with our developing understanding and knowledge about effective organizational change. Michael Fullan is particularly relevant in this context. He believes that in the current context the view of

> instructional or learning centred leadership as being central to successful development is no longer sufficient to meet the challenges of the rapidly changing context and the affect of the 'knowledge society'.
>
> (Fullan 2002b, p. 17)

The leader of the future must also be a 'cultural change leader' who is attuned to the big picture, a sophisticated conceptual thinker who is into transforming the organization through people and teams. He notes that

> transforming culture, changing what people in the organisation value and how they work together to accomplish it – leads to deep lasting change.
>
> (ibid., p. 18)

Fullan lists a number of essential atributes that characterize these cultural change leaders, including knowledge creation and knowledge sharing. In a subsequent article he develops the argument further and links cultural leadership to the importance of sustainability for organizations, and in particular schools, and the capacity of the organization to survive effectively in the future. He defines sustainability as 'the likelihood that the overall system can regenerate itself toward improvement' (ibid., p. 19). We would suggest along with other writers on the subject that practitioner learning is essential for regeneration and that collaborative enquiry is one of the most effective strategies for sustaining practitioner learning.

Fullan puts the importance of relationships at the heart of successful cultural change and asserts that 'the single factor common to successful change is that relationships improve. If relationships improve, schools get better' (ibid., p. 18). The process of collaborative enquiry is therefore doubly powerful. Collaborative enquiry requires colleagues to work together on the focus of their enquiry. In doing so they are not only creating and sharing knowledge and expertise; they are also developing positive professional relationships which make the whole organization a stronger and emotionally healthier place in which to work, and one where staff are better equipped to deal with the challenges they face in the twenty-first-century knowledge society.

Facilitative conditions for learning and teaching

School leaders have to ensure that teaching and learning is able to take place as effectively as possible in school. This means attending to the ethos of the school and the systems and processes which the school has in place to ensure that they support and do not hinder the core process of the school, namely the learning and teaching. A school that had facilitative conditions in place would be one where:

- the school leaders model collaborative enquiry;
- there are opportunities for teachers to meet and work together in non-hierarchical groups;
- the design of the timetable and other structures and processes are such that it is possible for different groups of practitioners to meet and learn together about collaborative enquiry;
- there are opportunities for both formal and informal dissemination of the learning;
- good internal communication systems are in place;
- the school has good external networks to other practitioners and researchers and actively encourages and enables their work and experience to be shared in the school;
- a culture has been developed that encourages and supports debate.

The importance of school leaders developing these 'facilitative conditions' is discussed further in Chapter 2.

The development of learning-centred leadership

Leadership for authentic school improvement must have as a core focus the need to enhance the learning and teaching. A school leader cannot do this on his/her own. To do that effectively the leadership of the learning and teaching must be shared and must permeate the whole staff. Collaborative enquiry, as the examples in this book illustrate, encourages a more distributed form of leadership. In this sense it also becomes a 'democratizing' process.

David Jackson (2000) describes some of the main characteristics of this dispersed, or distributed, leadership model. They include multilevel leadership built around shared values, empowerment and active democracy and a belief in collaborative learning as a source of leadership capacity. Collaborative enquiry and collaborative learning imply participation from all levels in the school community and as such it is an 'actively democratic process'. The leaders of enquiries were often deliberately chosen from more junior members of staff.

The concept of distributed leadership is explored further on page 65.

The importance of developing 'learning enriched' schools where CPD is planned and designed to enhance both pupil and practitioner learning

It was Susan Rosenholz (1989) who used the term 'learning enriched' schools to describe schools where ongoing learning of practitioners was taken for granted as a necessary aspect of their professional life. Schools who are creating 'learning enriched' environments for both pupils and practitioners make professional learning a priority activity for their staff. They will usually have moved away from more traditional models of 'in-service training' and off-site, one-off courses to a more developmental and sustained approach, more grounded in the work of the school and its practitioners and, more often than not, school based. The school and its staff will have taken control of their own learning and will be designing the professional development opportunities to meet both individually identified needs and interests as well as those of the organization as a whole. The approach will be more explicitly 'on the job', will involve staff collaborating with each other on aspects of practice. In addition, opportunities will have been created for this to happen. Whilst there may well be a need for some of the more 'traditional' activities, such as specific off-site courses, the choice will be more discriminating and even if no collaboration is planned into the design of the course, the school itself will ensure that there is a collaborative process in place in the school for the learning to be shared and built on.

It is important to note that there is no implication that 'new knowledge' is not welcomed in these learning enriched schools – it is. But the practitioners will have thought carefully how best to introduce and work with that new knowledge in the context of their particular school. Indeed 'learning enriched' schools make a conscious decision to seek out new knowledge and current research for their own purposes.

For example, one school has given an extra responsibility point to a member of staff for 'Research'. Her role is to maintain an up to date knowledge base about relevant new research, make a selection from that research in the light of the school's current needs and then to establish collaborative groups of staff to consider the research and design ways of testing it out in their own context to see if it has anything to offer. Another school has built 'enquiry and research' into their Performance Management Review (PMR) processes.

These schools have encouraged and created opportunities for staff to engage with each other in a deeper professional dialogue about current practice. In these schools staff are:

- keeping the focus on pupil learning;
- working collaboratively with other colleagues on aspects of pupil learning;
- using existing research to stimulate their own thinking and practice;
- engaging in enquiry themselves;
- often seeking feedback from pupils about their learning;
- sometimes working with an external consultant or adviser.

The leaders in the schools are organizing time so that it is possible for staff to work together on enquiry activities. The development of enquiry is a powerful strategy to support practitioners and make the concept of 'informed professionalism' live. Reed and Street, writing in the Research Matters Series, note the following.

> We have identified four particular evaluative capabilities that can develop as a result of engaging in reflective enquiry in classrooms and which lead to evaluation for learning. Practitioners can:
>
> - Generate questions amongst themselves and with pupils about learning;
> - Engage in regular dialogue to find out more about pupils' experience and orientation to learning;
> - Develop a critical interest in current research about learning and use it to reflect on their own practice;
> - Be willing to stand back from their own situation and use evidence more systematically to come to new conclusions about the reality of what is happening in their classroom rather than basing their work on unexamined assumptions.
>
> (Reed and Street 2002, p. 7)

David Hargreaves (2003) has explored the development and sharing of practitioner learning in a discussion pamphlet for the 'think tank' Demos. In it he considers the implications of the government's transformation agenda, with particular reference to practitioner learning.

The transformation agenda and cultural change leadership and sustainability

The 'transformation agenda' is the third aspect of the external context for enquiry that is important to explore. David Hargreaves (2003) considers what the concept of transformation might mean and how such transformation of the education system can be achieved. He argues that 'transformation could occur by shaping and stimulating disciplined processes of innovation within the school system and building an infrastructure capable of transferring ideas, knowledge and new practices laterally across it' (p. 12). He quotes Revan's law: 'For an organisation to prosper, its rate of learning must be at least equal to the rate of change in the external environment'. He observes that 'as the rate of change accelerates outside this country, schools and the DfES must improve their capacity to learn' (p. 21).

The big challenge for systems like education is to work out how to learn from themselves. Hargreaves discusses the difficulty the education system and schools in particular have had in sharing and disseminating not simply 'good practice' but ideas and knowledge across and between schools and their practitioners. His belief is that the transformation agenda depends upon 'human interaction, as education requires millions of people to change their behaviour and in return this requires some different if complementary strategies' (p. 18–19).

Developing the practice of professional enquiry amongst practitioners is one of those strategies. He emphasizes the need for 'disciplined innovation' – innovation that is focused and bounded. The same applies to collaborative enquiry. A school or network needs to have a small number of sharply focused enquiries rather than spreading the enquiry work too thinly.

Intellectual, social and organizational capital

David Hargreaves identifies three types of 'capital' which are essential when developing a community of enquiry in schools and when building a school's capacity to manage the process of change and, in particular, to take control of it.

- Intellectual capital is the human capital in an organization. An effective and empowering organization will use and mobilize this to good use.
- Social capital is the cultural and structural capital in an organization. It is about the trust that is generated between people working together and the quality of the network developed.

- Organizational capital. This refers to the colleagues in schools, particularly those in leadership roles. Their capital is their knowledge, skill and ability to improve the school and make the best use of the intellectual and social capital.

The process of developing a community of enquiry is an effective strategy for ensuring that the best use is made of the intellectual and social capital in a school. Collaborative enquiry is an important strategy to develop as the process itself is a 'community of enquiry' in action and this will further develop and strengthen the community of enquiry in the school. Hargreaves acknowledges that developing communities of enquiry takes time and effort but he believes that this is time well spent when compared with the amount of time and energy that has been wasted in the past on transferring 'what does not work'. He notes that 'transferred innovation is a simple idea, but moving knowledge is a difficult practice' (David Hargreaves 2003, p. 41).

Ways in which capacity building in an organization supports collaborative enquiry

Capacity building is core to the 'transformation agenda' and both a process and an outcome of collaborative enquiry. One of our main reasons for advocating that schools and the staff in them consider engaging in collaborative enquiry processes is that it is an effective way of working to build individual and organizational capacity. Because the notion of capacity is so central to the rationale for collaborative enquiry, and because it is notoriously difficult to define easily, we have set out here what we believe it means and how it is developed.

In this case the capacity we are talking about is the capacity to manage change, respond positively to new challenges and to be able to develop, reflect on and refine professional practice to support continued development. Stoll, Fink and Earl (2003) discuss the need to enhance capacity from both the inside and the outside. Collaborative enquiry enables a school to do both because the practitioners involved will be looking beyond their own school to engage with the research and knowledge base that already exists elsewhere. To do this they will almost certainly be working with external colleagues who will provide support for the research and enquiry process. Stoll and colleagues believe that internal capacity building includes: believing in success; making connections; attending to motivation; understanding and experiencing emotions; engaging in community; enquiring; creating; practising and finding time. Enhancing capacity from the outside includes: recognizing the importance of learning for all; respecting and promoting professionalism; supporting continuous learning; getting to know your school; understanding that all schools are not the same; creating new designs for working with and networking schools; offering critical friendship and developing deep learning.

The reason for developing this capacity is because schools need to be able to sustain change and development over time. Stoll *et al.* identify some aspects of organizational life and some ways of working that need to be 'attended to' if capacity is to be developed. These include the importance of leaders:

- ensuring that everyone is enabled to contribute and is expected to contribute;
- developing ways of working that encourage and enable staff to work with each other – the development of networking (which is explored later in this book);
- making sure that colleagues' motivation is supported and encouraged, as people can only grow and develop if they are motivated to do so;
- giving time to help members of the community develop their own emotional literacy capacity, because good emotional relationships are essential for growth;
- working together with colleagues to build a sense of community;
- developing an enquiry approach to the practice of learning and teaching;
- encouraging creativity amongst the staff;
- being prepared to practise! New ways of working and learning take time.

The NCSL commissioned research (Hadfield *et al.* 2002) into the notion of capacity building, and drew from the existing literature and research and from their own work with 50 school leaders discussing their understanding of capacity. The working definition they use states

> capacity is a measure of the generative potential of a school to improve, manage change and sustain development.

> (p. 12)

It is the power and ability to grow.

They quote the Hopkins *et al.* (2001) definition of capacity as 'the collective competency of the school as an entity to bring about effective change. This implies four core components: knowledge, skills and dispositions of individual staff; a professional learning community in which staff work collaboratively; programme coherence; technical resources' (p. 6).

Figure 1.2: School, individual and team capacity

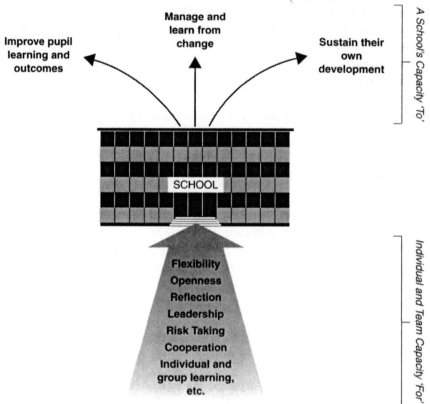

Hadfield *et al.* in the NCSL research distinguish two ways in which the notion of capacity is currently used in schools: 'a general ability or potential of a school to improve pupil outcomes, manage and learn from change, and sustain their own development' (p. 8). And 'the types of knowledge, skills, attitudes, and relationships required of individuals and teams within a school that underpins its development' (p. 8). To avoid confusion around these two levels they are presented diagrammatically.

As the diagram shows it is the people in the organization who need to develop capacity, and to do this they need to develop a set of characteristics, qualities and skills. The process of collaborative enquiry develops all three aspects.

The starting point of this chapter is that top-down reforms are no longer sufficient to guarantee the continued growth and development of individual schools, and that the continued development and growth depends on individual schools finding their own way forward. Capacity building becomes essential under these circumstances.

Mitchell and Sackney (2000) believe that

> Organisation capacity for a learning community implies that schools are structured to support connection rather than separation, diversity rather than uniformity, empowerment rather than control, and inclusion rather than dominance. ... Building organisational capacity, then, means paying attention to the socio-cultural conditions, the structural arrangements, and the collaborative processes in the school.
>
> (p. 78)

The ways of working illustrated in the examples in this book provide examples of leaders in schools developing ways for staff to work together on collaborative enquiry to develop their capacity for ongoing professional learning.

In discussing the link between capacity building through professional learning and school improvement Mitchell and Sackney observe that 'there is overwhelming agreement that professional learning, although not a magic bullet, is directly linked to educational improvement and school development' (ibid., p. 15).

How has your understanding of the concept of 'informed professionalism' been enhanced by your reading of this chapter?

Summary

This chapter has focused on explaining what collaborative enquiry is and discussing why it is an important and timely concept. A summary of the main points discussed in the chapter under each of the two questions is given here.

What is collaborative enquiry?

- Collaborative enquiry is a particular type of school-based research. The particular characteristics of collaborative enquiry include: practitioners working with other colleagues to research aspects of their practice together to an agreed focus; practitioners drawing on the current knowledge and research base and working with and integrating that with their own knowledge and experience; and practitioners often working with an external colleague from HE who supports the enquiry process. Sharing their knowledge and learning in an ongoing way is a key element of the process in order to make that knowledge available easily to colleagues beyond the group.

- Collaborative enquiry is a form of research, but the definition of research is not straightforward and the notion of collaborative enquiry as a form of research is contested.
- Collaborative enquiry is sometimes described as 'good enough' research but this does not mean it does not have rigour. The research criteria from the National Teacher Research Panel have been included (p. 38) as an example of rigour for practitioner research.
- In essence the process is a group of peers facilitating learning for each other.

Why is collaborative enquiry an important concept at this time?

- There is an emerging consensus that the top-down reform initiatives are not sufficient as a long-term strategy to support continued development and improved performance in schools.
- The political context has shifted towards 'informed professionalism' and a belief that schools will need to find their own ways to respond to the challenge of the knowledge society and the twenty-first century.
- There is shift towards cooperation not competition between schools which will support the development of collaborative enquiry across schools.
- The nature of and understanding about effective CPD is changing with more of the opportunities being site-based and directly linked to school practice and priorities.
- Because it is based on a belief that teaching needs to be a research-informed profession with practitioners being encouraged to relate to and use current research about learning and teaching.
- There are proven benefits to practitioners and their pupils of engaging in and with research. These include: the encouragement of more reflective practice; enabling colleagues to engage in a more professional dialogue with each other; and making possible a rigorous discussion of learning and teaching which is based on research evidence.
- Collaborative enquiry is a core strategy for continued school improvement and transformation, it is essential for 'authentic' school improvement which puts the central responsibility on individual schools to manage the demands of a knowledge society, developing professional learning communities.
- It is essential if the 'transformation' agenda is to be successful and if schools are to be able to develop their intellectual, social and organizational capital.
- It helps to build individual and organizational capacity.

To what extent are the characteristics of 'authentic' school improvement in place in your school or organization?

What progress has your school or organization made towards being one that is 'learning enriched'?

How would you assess: Your own capacity to learn? Your school or organization's capacity to learn? Your school or organization's capacity to innovate?

References

Cordingley, P. (2003) 'Research and evidence-based practice: focusing on practice and practitioners', in Lesley Anderson and Nigel Bennett (2003) *Developing Educational Leadership: Using Evidence for Policy and Practice*, London: Sage Publishing.

Earl, L., Watson, B., Levin, B., Leithwood, K., Fullan, M., Torrance, N. with Jantzi, D., Marshall, B. and Volante, L. (2003) *Evaluation of Implementation of National Literacy and Numeracy Strategies*, Toronto: Ontario Institute for Studies in Education, University of Toronto.

Fullan M. (2002a) Report to the DfES, August.

Fullan, M. (2002b) 'The Change Leader', *Educational Leadership*, May 2002.

Galton, M. (2002) Final Conference of the TTA Research Consortia.

General Teaching Council (England), Work in progress 2004

Hadfield, M., Chapman, C., Curryer, I. and Barrett, P., (2002) *Building Capacity, Developing Your School*, Nottingham: National College for School Leadership.

Hargreaves, A. (2003) *Teaching in the Knowledge Society*, Oxford: Oxford University Press.

Hargreaves, D. H. (2003) *Education Epidemic Transforming Secondary Schools Through Innovation Networks*, London: Demos, pp. 21–2.

Hiebert, J., Gallimore, R. and Stigler, J. W. (2002) 'A knowledge base for the teaching profession: what would it look like and how would we get one?' *Educational Researcher* 31 (5), 3–15.

Hopkins, D. (2001) *School Improvement for Real*, Falmer: Routledge.

Hopkins, D., Beresford, J., Jackson, D., Singleton, C. and Watts, R. (2001) *'Meeting the Challenge'* – *An Improvement Guide for Schools Facing Challenging Circumstances*, Nottingham: University of Nottingham (quoted in *Building Capacity, Developing Your School*, p. 6).

Hopkins, D. (2003) NAHT Secondary Headteacher Conference.

Jackson, D. (2000) 'The school improvement journey: perspectives on leadership', *School Leadership and Management* 20(1): 61–78.

Joyce, B. and Showers B. (1988) *Student Achievement Through Staff Development*, London: Longman.

Mitchell, C. and Sackney, L. (2000) *Profound Improvement Building Capacity for a Learning Community*, Lisse, The Netherlands: Swets and Zeitlinger.

Reed, J. and Street, H. (2002) 'School self-evaluation: a process to support pupil and teacher learning', *Research Matters* 18, National School Improvement Network, Institute of Education.

Rosenholz, S. J. (1989) *Teachers' Workplace: The Social Organization of Schools*, New York: Practitioners College Press.

Saunders, L. (2002) 'Evidence-informed teaching: the appliance of science of pedagogical transformation? A view from the GTC', paper supporting a presentation given at the joint PARNE/Evidence Network Seminar on 'Integrating Evidence Based Practice with Continuing Professional Development'.

Stoll, L., Fink, D. and Earl, L. (2003) *It's About Learning and It's About Time*, London: Routledge.

The ESRC Teaching and Learning Research Project, *www.tlrp.org*

National Teacher Research Panel

Research Criteria

Key criteria for assessing research which is intended to be useful to teachers are summarized below.

Projects need:

1 A sharp focus, supported by clear research questions or proposals for developing them. Projects should be directed towards outcomes which can be communicated to and used by teachers to inform their classroom practice.

2 Convincing arrangements for accessing and building upon what is known already about the area to be studied. Projects need to show that they will make a systematic and cumulative contribution to what is known already about effective teaching of the curriculum and/or pedagogic leadership.

3 Clear research methods. Projects need to show that they:

- will take place in a relevant field of investigation;
- include practical and systematic arrangements for collecting evidence that is relevant to the research question or hypothesis. They will need to show that:

  - interview or observation goals are clear;
  - their evidence is relevant to the experience of teachers;
  - the collection analysis and interpretation of data will be guided by a consistent logic;
  - there are clear strategies for triangulating data. For example, are data about processes complemented by data about outcomes? Are data about perceptions complemented by observation data?

- have practical arrangements for checking the interpretation of evidence and findings with practitioners and researchers;
- involve systematic approaches to analysing data which allow the testing of issues emerging from the data as well as exploration of original hypotheses.

4 Details of arrangements for communicating the research to others, including for example:

- arrangements for working out the meaning or the implications of findings for day-to-day practice with teachers;
- a report or other materials for publication in, for example, professional journals, LEA newsletters, research journals, preparation of a video or interactive CD ROM as well as reports which enable academic peer review;
- a short summary designed to whet teachers' appetite for finding out more and to enable them to make an informed judgement about whether the research is relevant to their needs;
- the development of vivid exemplification of ideas, theories and approaches being applied in practical teaching and learning contexts.

Previewing Chapter 2

Chapter 2 offers an extended discussion of the key characteristics of collaborative enquiry. These expand the general definitions given in Chapter 1. The chapter develops further the arguments for why it is an important concept at this time, by showing how collaborative enquiry makes a difference to practice. The concept of learning organizations, introduced in Chapter 1 is explored in detail in Chapter 2 and extended into consideration of professional learning communities. The reasons why collaborative enquiry is effective as an adult learning strategy are discussed.

The facilitative conditions which were introduced in Chapter 1 are analysed in more detail by focusing on the implications of collaborative enquiry for school leaders and considering the importance of distributed leadership.

2 What does 'collaborative enquiry' look like?

David Jackson and Hilary Street

Chapter 1 provided an overview of the theory which underpins collaborative enquiry and a discussion of why it is an important concept at this time. This chapter extends the discussion to provide an overview of how the theory of collaborative enquiry manifests itself in practice.

This chapter seeks to answer the following questions:

1 What does collaborative enquiry look like?
2 Why does collaborative enquiry make a difference to practice?
3 Why is collaborative enquiry an effective adult learning strategy?
4 How does collaborative enquiry happen within or between schools?
5 What are the implications for school leaders?

1. What does collaborative enquiry look like?

There are some particular characteristics of collaborative enquiry which are important to note because it is these characteristics that make it such a powerful tool to enhance practitioner learning and to improve and enrich the learning experience of pupils in classrooms.

The characteristics of collaborative enquiry include:

- taking the current school context as the starting point;
- problematizing the day-to-day work (not making assumptions about what is going on, but questioning what is taken for granted);
- building out from what has gone before and what is already known;
- the links with Higher Education;
- engaging in a process of investigation that is rigorous and disciplined in relation to purpose;
- ensuring that data gathering and analysis are understood by all involved to be an essential part of the process;
- the process of knowledge creation;
- representing findings in such a way that they can be accessed by other practitioners.

Taking the current school context as the starting point
A core message in the school improvement literature is that in order for any school to go forward effectively it has to have a clear understanding of 'where it is now'. This ensures that the decisions it makes about intervention strategies are grounded in and informed by the unique context of the school. The first activity, then, when seeking to develop and improve a school or network is to find out more about current practice in relation to the particular area of enquiry.

One school, for example, wanted to enquire into how teaching assistants could be involved more effectively as an additional learning resource in the classroom. To explore the current context they invited a trusted outsider to interview each of the teaching assistants in order to gain their perspective on their current role in the classroom. The outsider also undertook some classroom observations and spoke to small focus groups of pupils to obtain their perspective. They also looked at relevant documentation such as practitioner planning. The results from the initial audit (enquiry) highlighted a number of questions for further exploration and identified particular aspects of the role of the teaching assistant that the teachers and teaching assistants wanted to enquire about together. Interestingly, the audit also modelled some of the processes for enquiry: enquiry methodologies, valuing voice, building constituency, etc. Without the clear analysis of the current situation, which emerged from the investigation of the current context, the school may not have been enquiring into the most strategically important part of the role, or have been starting from where they were.

Problematizing the day-to-day work (not making assumptions about what is going on, but questioning what is taken for granted)
Collaborative enquiry deliberately problematizes the work of the school, by posing questions about aspects of practice which may benefit from being 'enquired into' and explained and understood further, before deciding on what action and interventions may be appropriate to support future development or to address issues identified. For example, a group of staff from a number of secondary schools who each had a Best Practice Research Scholarship (BPRS) to investigate effective learning and teaching at AS/A2 level worked together on the enquiry. They were all initially surprised at how much time was needed at the planning stage to articulate what precisely their concerns were and what specifically they could enquire into. This process meant that the enquiry work was fine tuned and honed from the beginning.

It is important to note though that enquiry is not necessarily a 'deficit' model. An enquiry does not have to be about something that is 'wrong' or 'not working correctly'. It has been said that good practice in the classroom is one of the best kept secrets, and yet for a school wanting to go forward unlocking and using that resource can have a powerful impact on other staff and pupils. One school in challenging circumstances was working within a network of schools committed to collaborative enquiry (the outcomes of which were then shared between schools). The school was having difficulties making an enquiry into student motivation and learning behaviour take off. Staff were demoralized by the enquiry, which seemed too large and too pervasive. When it was suggested that the focus was both reversed and narrowed, things changed. The fundamental questions became 'Where in the school are pupils highly motivated and exhibiting positive learning behaviours? What is going on there that is widely transferable?' Almost immediately the process was more successful – both as an enquiry and as a process that created a climate receptive to the outcomes of the enquiry.

An enquiry about good practice such as this might ask:

- Where is the current best practice in the school or network?
- Why do we consider that to be best practice?
- How did it develop in that way?
- Which classes seem to motivate students most?
- What factors seem to explain why that is the case?
- What can we learn from that? What principles can we derive that could be applied more widely?

Building out from what has gone before and what is already known

One of the characteristics that gives rigour to the type of school-based enquiry discussed in this book is that the processes of enquiry build from, and include, understanding about the current research and evidence of the topic or issue being explored. In the examples given later in this book, finding out about existing research was an integral part of the way of working. In one example the network specifically employed a researcher part of whose brief was to enable staff involved to have access to relevant research literature. In another school studied, one of six collaborative enquiry groups established around the school's improvement priorities was a 'knowledge management group'. It was charged with the responsibility of ensuring that the other five groups had the papers, articles and research findings that would inform their work; that the work of the other five groups was constantly available and shared with the wider staff (noticeboards, intranet, newsletters, video clips, etc.) and that the groups had access to appropriate forums to share emergent findings (staff meetings, staff days, workshops, etc.). This proved to be an extremely important way of building enquiry from the publicly available knowledge base into everyone's work.

The links with Higher Education

A key feature of most enquiries is the relationship developed with HE and the explicit and self-conscious use of current knowledge and research about the particular focus of the enquiry. This active relationship with HE is one of the key ways in which rigour in the enquiry process can be maintained.

The examples given in this book show how the learning and practice being developed by enquiry groups integrated and drew on existing knowledge and understanding. If informed professionalism is to develop, then the link with current research and current effective practice has to be clear. Accessing current research and then having the time to think through what the implications of that are for practice is problematic. It has not been easy in the past for practitioners to access and use research findings easily. The Improvement in Action project led by the International School Effectiveness and Improvement Centre (ISEIC) is one example of how working with an HE colleague can give a structure and rigour to the teacher research and also provide a mechanism for accessing relevant research. The project aims to:

- refocus on pupils' learning and increase their active participation in the process of their learning;
- take an action research approach to a small learning-focused school improvement project;
- take time to develop together knowledge and understanding about learning and how school change and improvement actually works;
- reflect on the implications for the role of curriculum, school and LEA leaders in leading learning;
- draw conclusions about the impact of improved learning and teaching on standards and attainment.

Practitioners spend two days a term working with HE colleagues, and part of this time is used to consider relevant research and practice. The schools work together in small networks.

Engaging in a process of investigation that is rigorous and disciplined in relation to purpose

The pressure to act is one that bedevils much development work. It is tempting to decide quickly on an immediate course of action to be taken to address a perceived need that appears to be suggested by the enquiry data. A 'quick' response is not always the best one and may mean that the wrong cause is ascribed to a concern. Collaborative enquiry is a disciplined activity. It requires staff to take a systematic approach to the management of the process of enquiry, beginning with an enquiry about what research and evidence already exists that would help them take forward their own learning. Effective enquiry groups give themselves time to explore fully the aspect of learning and teaching which they have chosen to make their focus. Jane Reed and Caroline Lodge (2003), in a paper describing school-based practitioner-led enquiry with which they have been involved, discuss the dangers of the 'rush to act' when describing work that was developed with the practitioners. They emphasize the importance of 'delaying action and probing more deeply' into what is actually happening before deciding how to act.

Another quite similar example is given in Lorna Earl and Steven Katz's paper entitled 'Leading schools in a data-rich world' (2002). They describe a school's response to poor pupil performance in a large-scale maths assessment. The first response was that the practitioners needed professional development in the mathematics programme. However, by asking the question 'Do they do better in some areas than others?' (p. 13) it became clear that the issues lay in non-routine problems and in geometry. The next question, 'What kinds of difficulty are they having?' (p. 13) revealed two findings when test papers were analysed and enquiry undertaken with children and practitioners. The 'non-routine' issue was a literacy one – the language of the questions – the three-dimensional geometry – a practitioner one: the practitioners could not do the questions either!

Ensuring that data gathering and analysis are understood by all involved to be an essential part of the process

The gathering of rigorous and reliable data, either qualitative or quantitative or, where appropriate, both, is an essential part of the enquiry process and a necessary skill for colleagues to develop. In the context of collaborative enquiry where those participating are volunteers and where time and attention has been given to developing and nurturing trust and positive working practices as a group, then data becomes a tool to support thinking and action rather than, as has sometimes been the case in other contexts, a weapon to highlight deficiencies. Keating (1996), quoted in Earl and Katz (2002), explains it as follows:

> Inquiry is, very simply, a way of finding things out – collecting data and interpreting evidence in ways that enhance and advance understanding. Habits of mind incorporate dispositional, emotional, motivational and personality variables that contribute to competence in managing the environment and making decisions.

They go on to observe:

> We link inquiry to habit of mind to emphasise that this is a way of thinking that is a dynamic, iterative system with feedback loops that organises ideas towards clearer directions and decisions and draws on or seeks out information as the participants move closer and closer to understanding some phenomenon.

(p. 10)

It is only by actively engaging in a process of enquiry – of focused questioning and challenge of current practice – that new insights and ideas will be generated. New thinking cannot happen in isolation or in a vacuum. Earl and Katz (2002) observe that '... new insights don't happen by osmosis. They come from facing ideas that challenge the familiar ways of viewing issues. They happen in the dissonance and in the construction of new and shared meaning' (p. 18).

Although the focus of their paper is the skills that leaders need to develop in order to lead effectively, the discussion is in the context of leaders with a 'collaborative' orientation and with a belief in the power of collaboration both as a context for enquiry and as a means of liberating leadership. They conclude: 'The exciting thing about data is that it is so much more exciting when it is used collaboratively' (ibid., p. 22).

The process of knowledge creation

Enquiry in schools is a 'disciplined process that seeks to answer current or long-standing problems of practice, or that addresses deep issues or emergent questions' (Mitchell and Sackney 2000, p. 32). An example of a deep issue might be why, despite a whole range of interventions and a variety of different strategies for learning and teaching, a particular sub-group of boys in the school is still underperforming. An example of an emergent question might be 'how specifically does the use of interactive whiteboards enhance pupil learning?' Or even, 'Where in the school is it seeming to do this, and what is going on to enable this to happen?' Such enquiry processes are therefore ones which have the potential to create new knowledge about the focus of the enquiry that is useful to all staff in the school.

For example, two members of staff from a junior school spent 2002–3 using a group Best Practice Research Scholarship to work together to understand more specifically why it is that 'brain gym' appears to have a positive impact on pupils' learning. Their work focused at a whole-school level and they also undertook focused enquiry with specific groups of pupils with a range of special needs with whom they worked on a daily basis. As part of their research they 'engaged with the knowledge base' by researching what was already known about 'brain gym'. They also worked with an external advisor to reflect and make sense of their own learning from their practice; and, as a result, they were able to put forward some emerging hypotheses about the conditions, in their school context, for the effective use of 'brain gym'. One exciting finding was that these hypotheses seemed to travel, and they have proved useful as a starting point for other schools, too.

The important point to note is that the 'new knowledge' builds out from what is already known. For example, a headteacher of a primary school undertook an enquiry with a group of his staff to investigate the difference between pupils in KS2 with a 'performance' orientation and those with a 'learning' orientation in how they approached their studies. As part of that enquiry the practitioners concerned familiarized themselves with the literature that already existed on this area. Their first enquiry was to review the existing knowledge base. This provided a rich base from which to build and the hypotheses from which the enquiry questions could be drawn and applied within their school.

The example on page 48 illustrates the 'three circle' model which was described at the beginning of this book, it has been modified here to reflect this example.

It should be evident from the discussion of these characteristics, and from the examples offered, that the process of collaborative enquiry gives a central role to practitioners in creating and sharing knowledge and in the leadership roles surrounding the creation process and its use. The final characteristic, and a fundamental principle, of collaborative enquiry is that the 'learning' should be shared effectively with other practitioners.

Representing findings in such a way that they can be accessed by other practitioners

Sharing research with other practitioners who were not involved, so they can learn from and apply it, requires careful thought. It is not a straightforward process. Other practitioners need to choose to find out about the research. For them to make that choice the content needs to be important to them in their current context; they need to have a reason for wanting

Figure 2.1: The three fields of knowledge adapted to illustrate the primary example

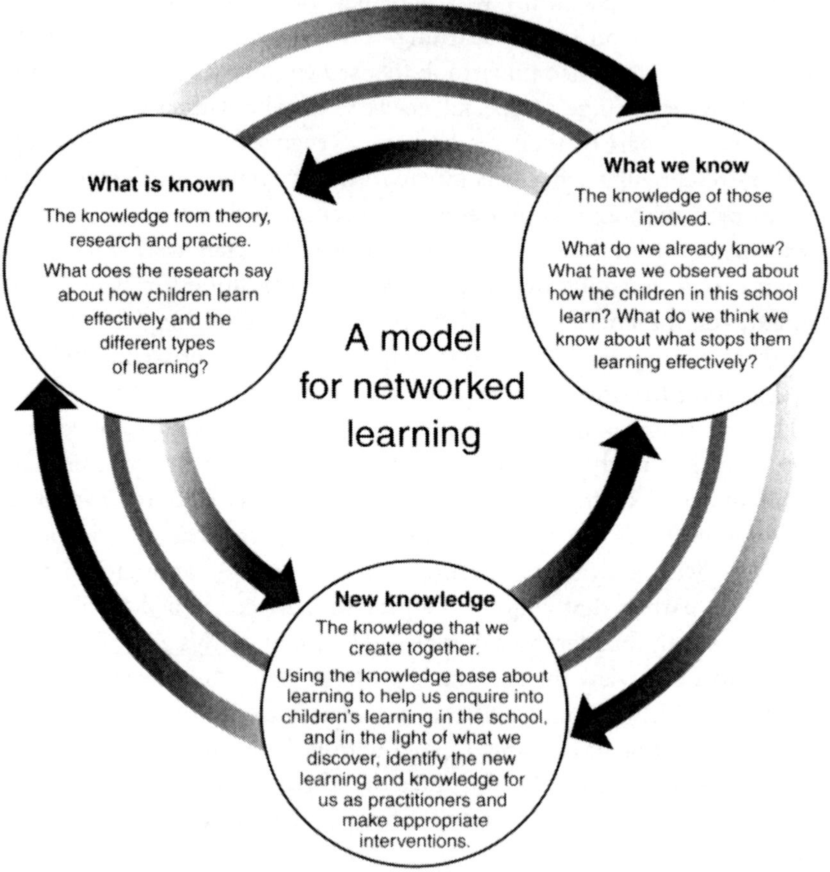

What is known
The knowledge from theory, research and practice.

What does the research say about how children learn effectively and the different types of learning?

A model for networked learning

What we know
The knowledge of those involved.

What do we already know? What have we observed about how the children in this school learn? What do we think we know about what stops them learning effectively?

New knowledge
The knowledge that we create together.

Using the knowledge base about learning to help us enquire into children's learning in the school, and in the light of what we discover, identify the new learning and knowledge for us as practitioners and make appropriate interventions.

to know more about the topic; they need to have faith that it will be useful to them, even though it may not be automatically transferable. Philippa Cordingley (2000) discusses the accessibility and usability of research and highlights the importance of the following if research is to be useful to practitioners:

- case studies that illustrate new approaches to widespread existing practice in vividly practical terms;
- sufficient detail of the teaching intervention or knowledge in action to enable teachers to test it out for themselves;
- sufficient detail about the starting point of the pupils and the communities, phases or subjects involved in the research output for teachers to see how their own pupils are similar to or different from those involved in the studies.

(p. 111)

It is also clear though that for teachers to use the research and evidence from others effectively, they need to be already gathering and using evidence from their own classrooms to give a context to this new information. For example, at one secondary school a group of teachers involved in collaborative enquiry as part of a network of schools used research evidence to identify an aspect of learning which would have value across all phases and pupils regardless of subject or year group. They chose effective group work. Group work was a classroom strategy which teachers were already using, but without sufficient training and support in how to manage it effectively. They worked together to develop their expertise in using the Kagan cooperative group-work strategies. The evidence of impact on practice included a positive impact on relationships; student to student, teacher to student and teacher to teacher.

What strategies do you currently use in your school to study and to share widely the knowledge about what is working well in your classrooms?

When you reflect on your current practice, what new learning have you personally gained about pedagogy in the last two years? To what extent have you shared this with colleagues?

Do the observations about data above help you reflect on how data is used in your school, or how it could be used?

How are you already using data to support the development of learning and teaching in your own practice?

2. Why does collaborative enquiry make a difference to practice?

This section summarizes the reasons and processes by which collaborative enquiry makes a difference to practice. It discusses:

- the central role of practitioners in collaborative enquiry;
- collaborative enquiry as an inclusive activity;
- the notion of 'real time' dissemination;
- the relationship with the culture of the school;
- the contribution of collaborative enquiry to the development of 'learning organizations'.

The central role of practitioners in collaborative enquiry

Collaborative enquiry puts practitioners at the heart of the professional learning process by giving them control over the decisions about what to investigate and by enabling them to enquire into matters of learning and teaching which are of importance and concern to them in their current role. As discussed earlier in this chapter, 'enquiry' is an important strategy for building the professional capacity of staff in a school. It makes them more able to manage the challenges faced by schools when responding to the demands of education and learning for the twenty-first century.

Practitioners have a central role in the knowledge-creation process. First, it is a significant and powerful professional development activity. Practitioners involved in enquiry are creators of knowledge and are also acting as 'facilitators' in the knowledge-creation process. In one of the examples given in Chapter 3, the practitioners were reflecting on how they currently taught thinking skills to their students and were working with their colleagues to analyse and refine their practices further. They were working together at residential activities, at development meetings, in reviewing videos of their classroom practice and acting as coaches to each other. It is also clear in the case study that they were enjoying engaging in these processes – were motivated and empowered. By doing so they were facilitating each others' learning as well as creating knowledge for wider use in their own school and beyond.

Colleagues who are engaged in enquiry ask questions of themselves, their colleagues and their students. They seek out new networks, ideas and practices. They experiment with new professional strategies in the classroom. As a group of staff working together on an enquiry, they formulate the new knowledge and then transfer and use this knowledge in their classrooms, and in so doing benefit directly the pupils they teach. The role and impact of the staff engaged in the enquiry goes beyond their own classrooms and is shared with the rest of the school community. In this way it is a leadership activity too.

Collaborative enquiry as an inclusive activity

Involving groups of staff in collaborative enquiry is an inclusive professional development opportunity. Because the focus is on their own practice and the professional discourse with their colleagues, the analysis arising will help practitioners adjust and develop their ways of working. Shared enquiry is by definition a social activity and as such it is an active and energizing experience, as the process of critical reflection takes place supported and challenged by others.

It is this direct link to practice in the classroom that makes 'enquiry' such a potentially powerful professional development strategy. The learning loop and the link with practice can be direct and immediate, which is often not the case in published 'academic' research. For example, in one of the case studies discussed in Chapter 3 it became clear that the plenaries in the 'thinking skills lessons' were an important part of the process and that a number of staff needed to develop their skills with plenaries further. Those staff involved had already identified that they wanted to enhance the learning from the 'thinking skills' and had engaged in a number of enquiry processes – videoing lessons, training sessions with external colleagues, discussion in the enquiry group. They were able to take the learning generated from those experiences and use it as the enquiry continued. They did not have to wait for 'the end' of the enquiry.

However, if the learning and the processes of the enquiry remain 'locked' in these groups there will be little impact on the rest of the school or network of schools. If the findings and learning from the enquiry process are significant enough, then the enquiry happening in two or three classrooms needs to be able to inform the practice of classrooms across the entire school and beyond.

In order for enquiry to have a wider impact, consideration needs to be given to the need to develop widespread ownership amongst the whole staff group right from the design stage. Finding a way to give the entire constituency (school or network) awareness and ownership of the collaborative enquiry process, rather than just delivering to them the product (the learning) from the enquiry, is a crucial factor in the success of collaborative enquiry activity. It is unlikely that a staff group presented with the results of someone else's enquiry will be influenced by the outcomes – sincere as the study group may be. For this reason school-based collaborative enquiry for school improvement should be a process whereby all staff are involved in the emergent process. In other words, there is a need to ensure that all staff understand that an enquiry is being undertaken, that the enquiry questions have meaning for the wider group and that the enquiry is being conducted for the benefit of all the staff and pupils in the school. There should be opportunities for input from staff at all stages of the enquiry. It is not just about collecting and studying data; it is also about valuing voice.

For example, a school with an enquiry group focusing on the use of an accelerated learning cycle might choose to begin with a focus on the core subjects, before planning ultimately to involve all subjects. At the end of the process they hope all subjects will be involved so they build in consideration of the end of the process at the planning stage. The enquiry group will a) have made sure that all staff know this particular enquiry is going on and understand why, and b) they will have put in place strategies to keep the rest of the staff body informed as the work progresses. One strategy the group might use to do this might be to invite one representative from each of the other subjects to work with them on their enquiry process and act as 'critical friends' in their group discussions when the group are designing the process or analysing their data. Alternatively they could invite other practitioners to help gather data or they could visit departmental meetings of the subjects not directly participating in the first round.

Enquiry leads to action

The purpose of enquiry is not only to create research or evaluation knowledge, but also to lead to 'action designs' and to implementation strategies within and across the school or network. Because collaborative enquiry is so grounded in the context of the school, the dissemination is simply part of the ongoing processes in the school with which people are familiar, and therefore not bolted on or externally imposed. It becomes an inclusive professional development and an ongoing growth activity for staff.

The notion of 'real time' dissemination

Unlike the time lag with some other forms of research, the dissemination of collaborative enquiry work takes place in 'real time', as the work takes place. The ongoing learning is feeding into practice all the time, both formally when the group meets to work together and analyse the data it is collecting and the thinking it is developing, and also often at an unconscious level as practitioners develop and fine tune their practice on a day-to-day basis, and as they engage in staffroom conversations with their peers. Not only is there no time lag between the research and the learning – because they are inextricably linked – the enquiry work itself is already based in the school and therefore the process of 'embedding' in practice becomes less problematic. This process of enquiry is an immediately useful activity to practitioners because it means that the information they are gathering is useful to them both 'at the point of collection' and when subsequently processed and synthesized. The fact that the information they collect is useful for them immediately is in itself a motivating activity.

For example, a Science department decided to ask all Year 11 students to do their own analysis of the mock exam paper, working in small groups (what was easy/hard/where did they have gaps in their notes for questions on the paper, etc.). This gave useful information to the pupils that informed their examination preparation – it was directly useful to them at the point of collection. For the practitioners, it provided data they could use immediately to inform the way they planned subsequent notetaking strategies and revision approaches, and it offered some generalizable points that the Science department (via a second year practitioner and her more senior peer mentor) was able to share with all staff at a subsequent staff meeting. However, this process also gave information that the department could use to help it choose the questions that it wanted to explore in the wider collaborative enquiry.

In 'good enough' research it is not the size or scale of the enquiry that is significant, but the quality of the knowledge generated. As enquiry findings turn into new teaching and learning practices with evidence of success, they are able to be shared more widely within the school or network as the examples in Chapters 3 and 4 illustrate.

An enquiry activity designed for school or network improvement purposes may only involve a small group of staff, but it can have wide implications if it is being undertaken by an enquiry group on behalf of the wider professional community of the school or network. In this way, enquiry gives rise to learning and to the application of that learning. Subsequent study of the implementation of new ideas gives rise to refinement and more robust findings – both about what works and about how to implement change. Leading the wider application of the learning within the school builds leadership capacity and spreads it more widely. It is a 'management of change' process, and the social dimension of collaborative enquiry is an ideal environment to tackle the 'implementation dip' that invariably accompanies change processes. The work of Stoll and Fink (1996) and Fullan (1993) make it clear that no process of change and development will proceed completely smoothly, for real change to take place there will almost certainly be setbacks and unexpected issues that arise. In a process of deep change things often get worse before they get better!

The relationship with the culture of the school

When undertaken successfully a process of collaborative enquiry develops the knowledge, skills and understanding of individual staff about the focus of the enquiry, and develops their pedagogical knowledge (e.g. the use of open questions to aid learning, how to develop collaborative group work in KS3). In so doing it has the potential to change their classroom practice and their understanding of the learning and teaching process. At the same time the working relationships between colleagues change and develop as a result of this way of working and in doing so contribute to a change in the school. We are using the word 'culture' here to describe *'the way we do things round here'.* In those schools where collaborative enquiry is supported and encouraged, there is an explicit intention to do things differently and to develop a culture, a way of working in school that:

- respects the contribution of all staff to the achievement of the school's aims;
- takes as a given that there is always more to learn about the complex task of learning and teaching;
- believes that it is important for staff as well as students to see themselves as learners and to model that for students;
- is committed to encouraging all staff, regardless of their formal role, to have the opportunity to take part in and lead an aspect of enquiry;
- believes that all staff need to continue to be 'researchers' in their own classroom;
- demonstrates a belief that any individual works more creatively and productively by working with others rather than on their own;
- takes it for granted that 'standing still' is not an option.

The contribution of collaborative enquiry to the development of 'learning organizations'

The school improvement literature includes a number of different lists and typologies which seek to encapsulate these characteristics of learning organizations (Stoll and Fink 1996; Sapphir and King 1985). The list provided by Stoll and Fink (1996) is a good example. Learning organizations:

- Treat teachers as professionals
- Promote high quality staff development
- Encourage teacher leadership and participation
- Promote collaboration for improvement
- Develop ways to induct, include and develop new organisational members
- Function successfully within their context
- Work to change things that matter
- 'Sweat the small stuff'.

(Stoll and Fink 1996, p. 150)

Many of the elements identified are the same as those encouraged and developed when staff in schools engage in a process of collaborative enquiry.

A number of reasons why collaborative enquiry is able to do this are listed below.

1 Collaborative enquiry is driven by an explicit learning and teaching focus and this means it:

- is likely to impact not only on practitioners but also pupils;
- has the potential to have an impact on individual pupils in individual classrooms;
- helps staff develop ways of working which also enable the learning to be shared across schools;
- is based on clear aims and shared professional values, which are aspirational and sharply focused on both teaching and learning (i.e. pedagogy not content);
- necessitates an openness to alternative ways of doing things;
- is based upon a belief in informed, creative and dispersed leadership which believes in continuous learning and actively promotes this amongst staff.

2 Collaborative enquiry is itself a continuing professional development process which:

- provides a way of working for colleagues that ensures they are not isolated and are supported in their professional reflection and analysis of their practice. Practitioners working together on enquiry activities create a 'learning context' for each other. They support and 'scaffold' each other's work;
- is developmental because it requires practitioners to visit theory and research in order to take forward their school-based practice;
- develops the skills of leadership across a wider group of staff and doing so enhances their professional expertise and boosts morale;
- is an energizing activity because colleagues are looking after themselves and each other professionally, and draw energy and enthusiasm from each other;
- demonstrates a commitment to improvement across the whole organization and an understanding of the wide range of activities that encompass professional learning;
- recognizes that learning occurs everywhere in the school (pupils, support staff, headteacher), often in diverse and unpredictable ways.

3 Collaborative enquiry is underpinned by working practices and processes which include:

- a willingness to engage with, and to learn from, theory and research;
- a capacity to share what the school knows about their practice and to act on what has been learnt;
- a willingness to create space, and especially time, for staff to innovate, with the security to make mistakes and learn from them; and to work in partnerships and flexible groups that come together for a specific 'enquiry purpose' and which enable professional learning to take place;
- use of external expertise to challenge thinking and extend the school and network's capacity to evaluate and to learn;
- high levels of communication, a shared language, joint solutions, collaborations, recognition, reward and celebration of success.

4 Collaborative enquiry contributes to the development of a learning culture in schools because it:

- enables the process of working collaboratively with colleagues on a shared aspect of classroom practice to be a supportive and stimulating experience;
- is generated internally by staff of a school and so is more likely to be 'embedded' into the work of the school;
- has no overtones of 'accountability' and as such is a liberating activity. Enquiry is an activity without blame. Data is neutral – the discourse of enquiry is different 'This is what we have found. What do you think it suggests we should do?' In particular the data collected is intrinsically useful to the staff collecting it. They can make use of it immediately in their ongoing enquiry work. It is 'useful at the point of collection' unlike in other research activities where the data is 'passed on' for analysis and then feedback is often given after a considerable time lag;
- is an inclusive activity open to all members of the teaching staff regardless of their role, and to support staff. In many schools it increasingly embraces pupils too;
- encourages and enables staff to work actively with quantitative and qualitative data that is generated and collected in the course of the enquiry and helps staff understand the use of data as a 'tool';
- offers a structural way to link individual professional development to the development of the organization as a whole.

The way colleagues work with each other in collaborative enquiry means it becomes a process by which practice can be transferred and developed. In this sense it is supportive of 'school improvement'.

From learning organizations to Professional Learning Communities

However, we would suggest that collaborative enquiry that is embedded in a school changes both the nature of the organization and the nature of its development. A school where collaborative enquiry is a way of life for staff is able not simply to continue to improve, but is able progressively to 'transform' both its practice and the type of organization it is. Collaborative enquiry describes a way of working which supports practitioner professionalism. It is predicated on an assumption that it is an essential activity for professionals to engage in because it will support the professional growth and development of practitioners and support the learning of pupils. Everyone will be a continuous learner when enquiry is a 'way of life' in the school.

The process of collaborative enquiry becomes 'metabolic' to the school. Enquiry is its preferred way of working and is used as part of the daily process of decision-making and solution generation. In this way it offers a constant frame of reference for staff in the school to use when trying to make sense of the demands and changes that are a constant part of the external context of the school. It becomes one of their strategies for responding to, making sense of and managing change. In this sense collaborative enquiry results in schools developing from 'learning organizations' to become 'professional learning communities'. Mitchell and Sackney (2000) explain the distinction in the following way:

> In a learning organisation, the fundamental values and cultural beliefs are most likely to be defined by the organisational elite, whereas in a learning community, they will be defined by the members of the community in negotiation with one another.
>
> (p. 6)

They provide a definition of a 'learning community':

> a learning community consists of a group of people who take an active, reflective, collaborative, learning-oriented and growth promoting approach towards the mysteries, problems and perplexities of teaching and learning.
>
> (p. 9)

It is when a school becomes a 'learning community' that transformation becomes possible. Collaborative enquiry has a part to play in that development. For example, in one secondary school where the headteacher had experience of leading an 'effective learning' research group with a nearby HE institution, she decided to develop a range of 'reflection oriented professional activities' with staff in her new school. There are 'teacher leaders' and 'resources leaders'. They are described as 'reflective practitioners' who act, lead and encourage the collaborative enquiry amongst practitioners. In addition to the enquiries themselves, the school is also examining how its capacity for improvement is being developed by the creation of such leaders.

One primary school in an LEA which works with a HEI to support learning communities across a number of schools, formed a number of 'collaborative enquiry teams' within the school, each team focusing on a different piece of classroom-based action research within an overall school focus. The staff took part in a number of professional seminars, network meetings and residential conferences, and consultancy HE partners helped the practitioners access the relevant research.

When you reflect on the distinctive characteristics of the culture of your school or organization to what extent would they be (or are they already) supportive of the process of collaborative enquiry?

To what extent are there aspects of the characteristics of collaborative enquiry, as discussed in this chapter, already in place in your school or organization?

What further action could you take to continue to develop your school or organization into a professional learning community?

3. Why is collaborative enquiry an effective adult learning strategy?

One of the reasons why collaborative enquiry is potentially such a powerful development tool is that it is appropriate to the needs of adult learners. It starts from where the learners are and takes their current situation, needs and concerns as the starting point for any learning. Collaborative enquiry is self-directed – individual staff choose to engage with the process, and it therefore builds on individual staff motivation. It is applied and relevant learning. It is also a respectful way of working with adults as it allows them to 'drive' the learning and decide together the learning processes that will be used. This does not mean that practitioners need to 'go it alone' in the learning process, indeed we would say that external support and facilitation were essential to support the process of collaborative enquiry. However, it is the practitioners working with the external facilitators and/or HE colleagues who have the central 'voice' in deciding how the learning will proceed.

This section considers:

- how our current and developing knowledge about effective learning in general 'fits' with collaborative enquiry as an effective learning strategy;
- the results of research into the effectiveness of collaborative CPD on teachers and students.

Current and developing knowledge about effective learning

Space precludes a detailed discussion of the current research base about effective learning, yet it is important to note the main themes because they give support to the belief that collaborative enquiry is an effective way of learning for adults (and also for children).

Multiple intelligences and individual learning styles

Recent work on multiple intelligences and individual learning styles has had a significant impact on the way teachers design the learning in their classrooms (Goleman 1996; Honey and Mumford 1986 and Gardner 1993). Those same insights apply equally to adults, who also bring a range of preferred learning styles and dominant intelligences to their learning. For example, in one school in which one of the authors was working recently, one of the practitioners in the group stated quite clearly and openly that he hated reading and found it difficult to learn well in that way. This colleague could clearly read and write adequately but his personal preference was to learn in other ways. The culture of the group with whom he was working was such that he felt at ease sharing his feelings. He also knew that they would be taken into account and inform the design of future group sessions. Collaborative enquiry is able to accommodate this range of styles and preferences because the practitioners themselves control the design of the processes to be used.

Learning as a social activity

An important development has been a much more explicit recognition that learning is a social activity. Most people learn more effectively with others than in isolation. Working with others offers the potential for 'checking out', explaining, teaching others, testing out the concepts and talking through our own understandings, misconceptions and uncertainties.

People construct personal understandings and build personal knowledge
bases at least partly through social interaction and social arrangements.

(Mitchell and Sackney 2000, p. 5)

A 'constructivist' approach to learning

In collaborative enquiry practitioners are able to make sense of their
learning together. They are also actively building knowledge together. This
'constructivist' approach to learning has become increasingly important
in our understanding of what supports effective learning and effective
learners (Watkins 2003; Carnell and Lodge 2002 and Claxton 2002).

A constructivist view of knowledge and learning emphasizes that
effective deep learning is not simply a process of transmission and
absorption. For deep learning to occur learners, in this case the practitioners, have to be able to work 'actively' with new knowledge and
insights, discuss, share and reflect with others, compare with their current
knowledge, understanding and practice, and modify and adjust both their
beliefs and practice accordingly. The fact that individual practitioners
are part of a group working together on collaborative enquiry is central
to this view of learning. Being a member of such a group enhances
motivation and engagement.

Mitchell and Sackney (2000) seek to explore how professional learning
takes place and how such learning connects to improved professional
practice. They quote the work of Louis, Toole and Hargreaves (1999)
and describe it as a 'wicked problem' that is 'inherently unpredictable and
chaotic'. They draw on the work of Gherardi (1999) which poses two
distinct types of learning. We have included that distinction here because
it is another illustration of the potential qualitative difference between a
learning organization and a learning community.

> An instructive way of addressing this wicked problem is found in Gherardi's
> (1999) distinction between learning in pursuit of problem-solving and
> learning in the face of mystery. The first is more instrumental and cognitive,
> the second more natural and intuitive. In her words 'Problem-driven
> learning was propelled by the aesthetic of the rational, while mystery-
> driven learning is sustained by the aesthetic of the relational' (pg 117). She
> claims that when professional learning is linked exclusively to problem
> solving and is pushed by institutional expectations, it loses its connection
> with the lives of the professional and runs the risk of being unnatural and
> ineffective. By contrast, when learning is linked to the mysteries of and
> perplexities faced by the professionals, it is embedded in the day-to-day
> context of the people and is more natural, effective and durable.

(Mitchell and Sackney 2000, p. 5)

Collaborative enquiry as an approach to learning has the potential to integrate both types of professional learning as the examples in the case studies in the next chapter show.

The results of research into the effectiveness of collaborative CPD on teachers and students

In 2003 the Evidence for Policy and Practice Information and Co-ordinating (EPPI) Centre undertook a systematic review on the impact of collaborative CPD on teachers' practice and pupils' achievements. This was an extensive study which highlighted the positive impact for teachers and their pupils of engaging in collaborative CPD opportunities (EPPI Centre 2003). The review found that in all but one of the studies they reviewed collaborative CPD was linked with improvements in both teaching and learning. Many of these improvements were substantial.

In relation to teachers they reported changes to teachers' behaviour which included:

- greater confidence amongst teachers;
- an enhanced belief in their power as teachers to make a difference to pupil learning (self-efficacy);
- an enthusiasm for collaborative working once they had got over initial anxieties about being observed and receiving feedback;
- a greater commitment to changing practice and trying something new;
- collaboration, which was important in sustaining change.

It is important to note that the positive outcomes sometimes only emerged after periods of relative discomfort – things often got worse before they got better.

The positive outcomes for students included:

- demonstrable enhancement of student motivation;
- improvements in performance;
- more positive responses to specific subjects;
- increased sophistication in responses to questions and the development of a wider range of learning activities in class and strategies for students. There were also some unanticipated outcomes in terms of change in attitudes and beliefs, enhanced motivation and increasingly active participation.

There was also sufficient evidence for the reviewers to identify some core CPD strategies that were used. They were:

- the use of external experts linked to school-based activity;
- observation;
- feedback (usually based on observation);
- an emphasis on peer support rather than leadership by supervisors;
- scope for teacher participants to identify their own CPD focus;
- processes to encourage, extend and structure professional dialogue;
- processes for sustaining the CPD over time to enable teachers to embed the practices in their own classroom settings.

All of these identified characteristics are of course present in a process of collaborative enquiry.

The ways of working described in the examples of collaborative enquiry in this book reflect many of these principles of good adult learning. For example, in the case studies described in Chapter 3 the staff involved were self-motivated; they were investigating aspects of pedagogy that were currently concerning them; they had autonomy to develop their enquiry within an agreed framework; their enquiry was firmly rooted in their specific school context, and they were personally motivated to engage in this professional learning.

Is the design of the current CPD opportunities in your school or organization informed by the principles of effective learning?

Do you find the EPPI Centre research quoted helpful when reflecting on effective CPD?

4. How does collaborative enquiry happen within or between schools?

The examples in this book are descriptions of professional learning communities. The key to developing learning communities through processes of collaborative enquiry lies in the collaborative study of practice. This involves engaging in collective enquiry (e.g. action learning sets, study groups, enquiry partnerships); making explicit the tacit knowledge of practitioners; formulating and conceptualizing together informed (or 'best') practice; sharing and learning from one another across the organization and between schools; reinventing practice together across this wider space; and coaching and supporting the application of new ideas to success. That is why we describe it as a metabolic process, a mode of being.

The development of collaborative enquiry through national programmes (such as the Networked Learning Communities) differ significantly from previous 'action-research' and 'school-based' research projects. One essential difference is in the detailed thinking that has been given to the scaffolding needed to support and sustain such activity. By 'scaffolding' we are referring to the systems and processes, the protocols and ways of working which the leadership and management of the school have implemented to enable collaborative enquiry to take place, and to enable the learning from the enquiry process to have an impact on the school.

At the launch conference for the NLC's programme in 2002, Lauren Resnick made the following observation about networked learning and collaborative enquiry:

> It's not about working harder, it's about working smarter. There are certain kinds of intellectual engagement that if you really work hard at, even if you're not good at yet, will actually make you smarter. An intelligence building environment will coach you in using problem-solving skills. It will praise you, but it will also hold you accountable. All of this is about organising for this new kind of effort. We can take this organising effort idea and use it to think about how our classrooms are organised, how our schools are organised, how our networks are organised.
>
> You can only legitimately expect people to engage in continuous learning if you agree to the concept of two-way accountability. It's not just that they are accountable to you for better and better teaching, it's that you are responsible to them. They can hold you accountable for their opportunity to better learn and practise their craft. The system is responsible for providing the opportunity to learn. If it won't provide that then it can't expect accountability to its demands.

How far do you already link with other schools or organizations for CPD? Could this be developed further into more focused enquiry activities?

5. What are the implications for school leaders?

This concept of 'reciprocal accountability' described by Lauren Resnick is an important one for school leaders. Pressure without support will not deliver the change and development necessary. The system is asking more from schools and from school leaders in terms of 'raising the bar and closing the gap' of achievement. School leaders in their turn are increasing their expectations of their staff. It is the leaders who have the responsibility to create the enabling conditions for collaborative enquiry and sustained learning to take place in our schools. This section considers:

- what enabling structures for enquiry look like;
- the importance of distributed leadership for collaborative enquiry;
- what changes take place as a result of distributed leadership.

This means that leaders in schools have to recognize the importance of creating enabling structures for enquiry. A school's systems and processes are one of the mechanisms by which it can 'enshrine what it values'. If leaders in schools believe that collaborative enquiry and mutual and collective learning are important, then they have a responsibility to ensure that the school's working practices will facilitate this work.

What enabling structures for enquiry look like

The key elements of an enabling structure appear to be:

- the recognition that it is essential for someone to assume a coordinating function in order to sustain, energize and develop the work – it requires high-order leadership;
- a supportive leadership team who will think creatively about how to structure time to enable colleagues to engage in study and learning with one another, and time to engage with the wider staff and to share learning;
- adequate resources to support the development activities – this may involve access to equipment, buying in 'expert advice' or paying for colleagues to attend activities outside the school. It may also involve more creative resource support through timetabling, the appointment of new roles such as 'internal coaches' or 'lead learners';
- the opportunity for colleagues to have uninterrupted periods of development time at a residential course;
- tending to the culture which values and celebrates enquiry learning whilst also articulating a clarity of focus and direction (not exactly a structure but creating the climate and legitimizing the working practice);
- providing external support, as required.

Collaborative enquiry for school improvement is a high-level interpersonal and communication issue and as such is socially very complex. When a school is developing its work on 'collaborative enquiry' a number of colleagues will be involved in the process and managing that 'social' process is a part of the learning challenge – for 'formal' leaders and for participants. It takes time and skill to bring together a disparate group of people to explore the learning and teaching process with openness and rigour. As discussed earlier, staff involved need highly developed communication and interpersonal skills, as well as the capacity for intellectual rigour and reflection.

The importance of 'distributed leadership' for collaborative enquiry

One other part of the external context which has had a positive influence on the development of collaborative enquiry in schools is the development of the notion of 'distributed leadership'. There has been a significant shift over recent years in the thinking about leadership and management in schools (as well as industry). In contrast to the late 1980s and early 1990s when the notion of 'hero' leaders or 'charismatic' leaders appeared to dominate the agenda, the recent research into effective leadership has produced a more thoughtful and quite different approach to the task of leading schools. More recent work developed at the National College for School Leadership (NCSL) and elsewhere has focused on the concept of 'distributed leadership'. It is important to clarify what exactly the term means as it is important both in the development of collaborative enquiry and as an outcome of the process.

What change takes place as a result of distributed leadership

Distributed leadership is not simply a way of sharing out tasks amongst colleagues. It is an approach to leadership in schools which aims to involve many more staff in a leadership activity than is often the case in a conventional model of a leadership team. The concept of distributed leadership is based on an assumption that there are many more people with the potential to undertake leadership in schools than there are 'formal' leadership roles. Developing a way of working that 'distributes' leadership throughout the organisation is one way of making best use of the expertise that exists.

Nigel Bennett *et al.* (2003) in their review of the literature about distributed leadership for the NCSL noted that 'Drawing many people into the potential leadership group make it possible for initiatives to be developed from all over the organisation, and then adopted, adapted and improved by others in a culture of support and trust' (p. 3).

It follows, then, as we have indicated earlier, that a process of collaborative enquiry is an activity that can support the concept of distributed leadership in a school. The colleagues leading the collaborative enquiry do not have to be from the leadership team (though they sometimes are). Distributed leadership shares responsibility for aspects of the school's work more widely across the staff and also helps to develop a different set of social relationships between people. These relationships encourage and require a more open and trusting way of working with each other. This impacts positively on school culture and generates a way of working in which working groups are fluid, their life span is not indefinite and where all have a contribution to make. Bennett notes:

> A strong theme in the literature we studied emphasised fluid leadership, resting on immediate expertise rather than position, and enhanced through ad hoc rather than formally constituted groups, which may have to exist alongside them. Once again, this emphasises the need for relationships built on trust and mutual support. It also blurs the distinction that runs through conventional literature on leadership between leaders and followers.
>
> (p. 5)

The development of distributed leadership also requires the development of strong and effective team working skills. By opening up opportunities for practitioners across the school to engage in collaborative enquiry, the school is opening up opportunities for more practitioners to assume a leadership role in the process – to build teams, to focus on learning around school and classroom priorities, to contribute knowledge to the school's growth and to lead the implementation of new ideas arising from and within the enquiry process.

The work of Linda Lambert is particularly helpful in this context. In her paper 'Leadership capacity for lasting school improvement' (2003) she explores the relationship between leadership, learning and enquiry and offers a particular definition of the word 'community' which is useful in the current discussion. The word 'community' is often used imprecisely.

> Within the context of education the term 'community' has come to mean any gathering of people in a social setting. But real communities ask more of us than merely to gather together, they also assume a shared purpose, mutual regard and caring and an insistence on integrity and truthfulness. To elevate our work in schools to the level required by a live community then we must direct our energies and attention to something greater than ourselves.
>
> (p. 3)

Real communities are demanding. The case studies in Chapter 3 illustrate the level of commitment and trust required by colleagues engaging with 'enquiry'. As Lambert notes 'learning is at the heart of an effective and developing school community'. She also provides a 'health warning' – leadership for collaboration is a skilled activity.

> If we are distributing leadership in our schools and seeking to develop ways in which an increasing number of staff can engage in the leadership activity, then we have a responsibility to ensure they have the skills to undertake the process. It is not the fact of 'doing' leadership that develops the leadership capacity in school it is the 'skill' of doing it.

> Leadership capacity is developed at an individual level and as more become involved in it then developed at an organisational level as well. By leadership capacity I mean 'broad based' skilful participation in the work of leadership. By 'broad based' I mean that if the principal and a vast majority of practitioners and large numbers of parents and students are really involved in the work of leadership, then the school will most likely have leadership capacity that achieves high student performance.

> (ibid., p. 3)

A high degree of participation in leadership plus a high degree of skill results in a powerful force for change and innovation. Lambert writes that in such an institution you would see:

- principals, practitioners, parents and students as skilled leaders
  When people work together in reflective teams they make the most of their different talents and skills
- shared vision resulting in program coherence
  A shared vision based upon core values that the participants share is likely to be stronger than a 'principals' vision that needs to be 'bought into'
- inquiry-based use of data to inform decisions and practice
  School staff realise that they are the prime movers and leaders in the improvement process; decisions taken are likely to be 'better' decisions if they are taken after a process of enquiry that enables all members of the school community to have a voice and share their views
- Broad involvement, collaboration and collective responsibility reflected in roles and actions
  As individuals work together they change – there is usually a growth in feelings of collective responsibility
- Reflective practice that leads consistently to innovation
  This usually generates information (data) that informs thinking about practice in the future – for the better
- High or steadily improving student achievement
  In this context student achievement is seen as more than simply the raw attainment scores and staff are concerned to address the other 'student

learning' factors that affect performance, so that the gap between different groups of students is bridged and narrowed.

(ibid., p. 5)

Summary

This chapter has explored in more detail the characteristics of collaborative enquiry and its potential to make a difference to practice, in particular:

- operationalizing the 'idea' of collaborative enquiry by asking 'What does it look like?'
- summarizing the reasons and processes by which collaborative enquiry makes a difference to practice;
- identifying those characteristics that make collaborative enquiry an effective adult learning strategy;
- discussing the way in which collaborative enquiry takes place both within and between schools;
- considering the implications of collaborative enquiry for leaders in schools;
- discussion of the importance of gathering data systematically, sharing that data and using it to inform the process of the enquiry.

Key conclusions are:

- Collaborative enquiry takes the existing context as the starting point so that practitioners can relate their enquiry questions and consequent learning directly to their current practice and situation. It is a process which questions and problematizes the day-to-day work of learning and teaching. It does not make assumptions.
- Much of the theory and knowledge about how students learn effectively applies equally to adults. A constructivist approach to learning is particularly helpful for understanding that collaborative enquiry involves practitioners working actively with the knowledge base and current practice to develop thinking further.
- Collaborative enquiry is a social process and is complex to organize within or between schools. School leaders have to create the conditions that enable practitioners to work together easily.
- The concept of reciprocal accountability is crucial for school leaders who are trying to support collaborative enquiry. If leaders' expectations of the practitioners in the school are increasing then they have

to provide the right conditions to enable colleagues to meet those expectations.
- The development and extension of distributed leadership in the school is an essential feature of collaborative enquiry.

How have facilitative conditions for collaborative enquiry been developed in your school or organization? Could they be developed further?

How useful do you find the concept of 'distributed leadership' as a transformation strategy?

References

Bennett, N., Wise, C., Woods, P. and Harvey, J. A. (2003) *Distributed Leadership: A review of the literature*, London: NCSL.

Carnell, E. and Lodge, C. (2002) *Supporting Effective Learning*, London: Paul Chapman Publishing.

Claxton, G. 2002 *Building Learning Power*, Bristol: TLO Ltd.

Cordingley, P. (2002) 'Teacher perspectives on the accessibility and usability of research outputs', a paper presented by Philippa Cordingley and the NTRP to the BERA 2000 Conference, London, TTA.

Cordingley, P., Bell, M. and Rundell, P. (2003) *Dissemination for Impact*, London: NCSL.

Earl, L. and Katz, S. (2002) 'Leading schools in a data-rich world', Ontario Institute for Studies in Education, University of Toronto (OISEUT).

EPPI Centre (2003) 'How does collaborative Continuing Professional Development (CPD) for teachers of the 5–16 age range affect teaching and learning?', www.eppi.ioe.ac.uk.

Fullan, M. (1993) *Change Forces*, : London: Falmer Press.

Gardner, H. (1993) *The Unschooled Mind*, London: Fontana Press.

Gherardi, S. (1999) 'Learning as problem-driven or learning in the face of mystery?' *Organisation Studies* 20 (1): 101–24, quoted in C. Mitchell, and L. Sackney (2000).

Goleman, D. (1996) *Emotional Intelligence*, London: Bloomsbury.

Honey, P. and Mumford, A. (1986) *The Manual of Learning Styles*, Maidenhead: Peter Honey and Alan Mumford.

Keating, D. (1996) 'Habits of mind for a learning society: educating for human development', in D. Olsen and N. Torrance (eds) *The Handbook of Education and Human Development*. Cambridge, MA: Blackwell, 461–81.

Lambert, L. (2003) 'Leadership Capacity for Lasting School Improvement', Alexandria, VI: Association for Supervision and Curriculum Development.

Lodge, C. and Reed, J. (2003) 'Improvement in action: sustainable improvement in learning through school-based, teacher-led inquiry', Institute of Education London. A paper presented to ICSEI January 2004.

Louis, K. S., Toole, J. and Hargreaves, A. (1999) 'Rethinking School Improvement' in J. Murphy and K. S. Louis (eds) *Handbook of Research on Educational Administration*, 2nd Edn, pp. 251–76, San Francisco: Jossey-Bass.

Mitchell, C. and Sackney, L. (2000) *Profound Improvement Building Capacity for a Learning Community*, Lisse, The Netherlands: Swets and Zeitlinger.

Resnick, L. (2002) Extract from talk given by Lauren Resnick, The Institute of Learning, Pittsburgh at the Inaugural Conference for the Networked Learning Communities programme at Nottingham, June 2002.

Sapphir, J. and King, M. (1985) 'Good seeds grow in strong cultures', *Educational Leadership,* 42, March 1985.

Stoll, L. and Fink, D. (1996) *Changing our Schools*, Buckingham: Open University Press.

Watkins, C. (2003) *Learning: A Sense Maker's Guide*, London: Association of Teachers and Lecturers.

Whittaker, P. (1997) *Primary Schools and the Future*, Buckingham: Open University Press.

Previewing Chapter 3

Chapter 3 provides concrete examples for the elements of collaborative enquiry explored in Chapter 2 and shows through the examples how the leaders in the schools concerned were able to create the enabling conditions that made the enquiry possible. It addresses directly the question of how collaborative enquiry can happen within and between schools. The example from a primary school, a secondary school and a network clearly show how the process of collaborative enquiry had an impact on practice.

3 Enquiry in action

Julie Temperley and Julie McGrane

This chapter takes a thematic approach to case studies of instances where collaborative enquiry for school improvement has had major implications for participating schools and the practitioners and pupils within them. As the primary audience for this part of the book is likely to be practitioners and those establishing or leading collaborative enquiry in their own contexts, we have sought to provide sufficient operational detail for practitioners to decide whether activities could be adapted and used in their context or, where necessary, to help them to design their own approaches.

Three examples are used to illustrate ways in which key concepts and ideas were operationalized, how processes that supported implementation and learning were realized and what the outcomes were of those experiences from various perspectives. The examples are a primary school, a secondary school and a network of seventeen upper schools. Although both the primary and secondary schools were part of networks (and this was a significant factor in their experiences) the principal focus of these examples is on the opportunities created and impact achieved within the single school. In the explicitly networked example, particular attention is paid to the leadership and coordination necessary to make school-to-school connections so that each site could access learning from the others, as well as from its own enquiry.

The intention is to show that whilst the context and circumstances of individual schools are most certainly significant in the feasibility of collaborative enquiry as a strategy for school improvement – for instance in terms of scale, resources available and the amount of time that it takes to manage – collaborative enquiry can and does achieve the high aspirations set out for it in Chapters 1 and 2.

Following a short introduction to each example for orientation purposes, the chapter explores various phases in an enquiry process and examines how in each context those leading the enquiry connected the phases to their school improvement agenda, provided appropriate professional development and training for the practitioners involved and ensured that outcomes and findings were accessible and relevant for other practitioners and pupils.

The phases follow a broadly chronological sequence thus:

1 **Purpose:** identifying the issue to be addressed. *What's the enquiry for?*
2 **Context:** evaluating the state of readiness of the school and the individual participants. *What do we already know about the focus for the enquiry?*
3 **Planning:** clarifying the content for the enquiry. *What precisely is the question? What's already known 'out there' about it?*
4 **Operation:** leading and managing the enquiry. *Which practitioners and pupils should we work with? Who else needs to be involved? How do we share the outcomes?*
5 **Sustainability:** managing implementation and change resulting from the outcomes of the enquiry. *What will happen next?*

Collaborative enquiry rarely runs this smoothly and is more often experienced as a 'lumpy' and uneven process with dips, plateaus and, occasionally, dead stops. The examples reflect this. The practitioners involved are honest about the difficulties they encountered and generous in sharing their feelings about those difficulties and the solutions they reached.

Introduction to the examples

School A – the primary school

This primary school was the first school in its area to achieve Beacon School status following a successful Ofsted inspection in 1997. Having had no key issues in its last two inspections, the school was certainly in an enviable position, but this presented an enormous challenge to a school trying to maintain its own momentum and development. If all the systems, processes and ways of working that you would expect to see in an excellent school are in place, finding a strategy for sustained and continuing improvement requires a difference of approach. Supporting the professional learning of teachers in a challenging and creative way was the strategy chosen by the headteacher in this school.

The school had a culture of professional learning and they were used to being involved in 'new' thinking and development. One member of the practitioners held a DfES Best Practice Research Scholarship, one was on a panel for the development and trialling of Key Stage 1 test materials, one was a Local Education Authority (LEA) leading literacy teacher and three were leading numeracy teachers for the LEA. The whole staff was involved in the LEA's Emotional Intelligence pilot.

The school was part of an LEA network and a Networked Learning Community.

School B – the secondary school

This was a good and improving 11–18 secondary school in the north-east. It has been a Beacon School and Training School and has strong links with the local university. Sixty-three per cent of pupils at School B achieved GCSE A*–C in 2003, a 4 per cent improvement on the previous year.

The school was part of a Teacher Training Agency Research Consortium and later a Networked Learning Community.

The network

The network in this account was a coordinated group of seventeen upper schools (Years 9–13) in a single LEA who came together to learn about their individual schools, what works for teachers and students and what works in the support of school improvement at a networked project level.

The network began in October 1999 following research with upper school headteachers across the LEA into their aspirations for school improvement support. It was school-owned and supported by the LEA, match funded from school contributions and from the school improvement resources identified in the LEA's Education Development Plan (EDP). It also generated income through grants and scholarships to support particular strands of activity. The project team comprised a project manager, a research officer and a part-time administrator.

Amongst a superficially similar group of schools (seventeen large 13–18 comprehensives in a small county with a supportive LEA) there was a surprising range of cultures, attitudes to and understandings of professional development, school improvement, innovation and change. Acknowledging and celebrating diversity of experience became a strength of the project over time but this was carefully balanced with coherence building and conceptual clarity and frequent reference to a set of core values that came to be known as 'non-negotiables'. These were:

- a commitment to shared leadership;
- a focus on teaching and learning;
- valuing practitioner enquiry;
- engaging with best knowledge in relation to teaching and learning and school improvement.

When you reflect on the discussions so far, what characteristics of schools do you consider might affect their approach to collaborative enquiry?

What preparation do you feel would be needed in a school to create an environment in which collaborative enquiry might flourish?

1. Purpose: identifying the issue to be addressed. *What's the enquiry for?*

Successful leaders of collaborative enquiry look avidly for points at which the objectives and capacities built by any enquiry-related activity are congruent with existing priorities in schools. When it offers a strategy for practitioners to address challenges and even long-term problems identified by the school, by creating new avenues of opportunity, collaborative enquiry makes its best contribution to school improvement.

School A – the primary school

For the primary school, the big issue was transition from the Foundation Stage to Year 1. Both children and practitioners found the change from a play-based to a more formal curriculum a distressing experience. The school also had a concern about the underachievement of boys in Key Stage 2 (KS2), particularly in writing. The school was conscious of 'firefighting' in Year 6 and sought to make early interventions in Years 4 and 5.

There were also two subsidiary themes that the school wanted to permeate their work. In KS2 they planned to explore the use of ICT as a motivator and learning tool; to use ICT intelligently. They also aimed to use their enquiry work as a vehicle for the professional development of their middle managers and a way to design development opportunities for them.

This layering or 'nesting' of purposes is common to all of our examples and, whilst it is demanding of planning and management, it pays dividends in ensuring that each part of the enquiry is linked to and adds value to the other.

School B – the secondary school

During the early 1990s, the north-east of England became a centre for excellence in Teaching Thinking, centred on work at Newcastle University. This had helped generate significant commitment to Thinking Skills in the area where a growing number of passionate advocates were emerging in local schools. School B was one such school where this distribution of growing expertise and shared belief in the value of teaching thinking acted as a catalyst for activity.

The school had taken part in research at the university and TTA-funded teacher research on Thinking Skills and had focused specifically on the 'debriefing' part of a Thinking Skills lesson. That work had highlighted the fact that questioning skills were of great significance in effective Teaching Thinking. It was agreed, therefore, that at one level, the enquiry would focus on teacher and pupil questioning. It was hypothesized from earlier work on debriefing that effective use of open questions would encourage longer oral and written responses from pupils as well as facilitate greater metacognitive awareness, all of which have been shown to contribute to improving outcomes at KS4.

The school's commitment to Teaching Thinking and its status as a Training School meant that it identified as a priority the need to put appropriate professional development in place to enable practitioners to acquire the skills required for the delivery of effective Thinking Skills lessons. So a second question or layer in the enquiry became, *How do teachers learn to teach Thinking Skills – what has to happen to them and how does it feel?*

Finally, the school recognized a need to include an evaluative strand to their work and so set out to discover, *What impact does Teaching Thinking have on pupil learning?*

The network

For the network, two sets of purposes were in play; the network's and those of each individual school. At the project level, the network was in its second year and was gathering momentum steadily. However, the project team quickly realized that they needed to put in place structures that would help to sustain the work of the network beyond this initial period and looked for an intervention that would help each school to sustain their own enquiry and professional learning independent of the project team.

They identified peer coaching as a capacity-building school improvement strategy which would foster collaboration within each school and create a focus and demand for school–school collaboration across the network. They hypothesized that, in sharing their professional development with colleagues from other schools, participants would be actively engaged in understanding others and reflecting on their own organizational cultures; for example, attitudes to learning and to change; to challenges to traditional hierarchies and professional relationships and to classroom observation.

The network's enquiry focus was *What are the optimum conditions necessary in each school for coaching to have an effect on the range of teaching strategies?* and *How can structured peer support networks encourage teachers to develop their professional practice?*

Of course the network was in fact a group of individual schools who continued to function as such, even at the same time as being committed and active members of a network. So the same 'rules' about collaborative enquiry needing to be congruent with school development priorities applied. Below are just some of the purposes that the collaborative enquiry addressed for schools.

Network School W

The catchment area for this school had been changing dramatically as a result of new housing developments over the previous two years to the extent that the LEA was looking at building a new school to accommodate the growing population. In the event, it was decided instead to expand School W. The decision was taken very quickly and there needed to be a significant recruitment campaign to this already substantial school, resulting in a large intake of NQTs in the following September. The school identified peer coaching as an ideal vehicle for inducting these new colleagues into the enquiry culture of the school as well as fulfilling their obligation to NQT mentoring and enrichment. The trio recruited to peer coaching, therefore, were using the pilot year to refine their own skills and prepare for the following year when they would lead the induction and CPD programmes in school. (The school has since become a centre of excellence in provision for NQT and ITT and offers alternative provision to the LEA to which other schools in the network have access.)

Network School X

Simultaneous with the development of peer coaching was a move in school two to devolve management of the CPD budget for the following year to the School Improvement Group (SIG). This bold move on the part of the headteacher was designed to signal his commitment to enquiry-based CPD and to attach prestige to involvement in SIG activities to support them. A priority for the SIG was raising schoolwide awareness of and recruitment to Teaching Thinking following two participants' experiences in a previous collaborative enquiry. Peer coaching allowed the SIG to develop an alternative model for in-school development that involved collaboration and consultation across the whole school and a deliverable solution to the challenge of introducing Teaching Thinking into every department.

Network School Y

This school had a deep and abiding commitment to pupil participation in designing teaching and learning. From the beginning, colleagues involved had noticed one weakness in the models for Teaching Thinking, which was the lack of any feedback from the pupils about the experience. There was a formal debrief which enabled reflection on some of the learning from the process, however colleagues involved believed that there was a variety of other learning which pupils took from the Thinking Skills lessons. They identified this omission as an opportunity to combine their commitment to the pupil voice with the development of Thinking Skills strategies. They could then make a unique contribution to the network's understanding of the impact of Thinking Skills for pupil learning and to its knowledge about pupil participation in teachers' professional development. Peer coaching trios in this school, therefore, included a pupil who was trained in classroom observation and invited to participate as a full partner, apart from the delivery of lessons. As well as having one of the most exciting coaching programmes, classroom observation and feedback also became an intrinsic part of the schoolwide Students as Researchers enquiry: *What makes a good lesson?*

Network School Z

This was an undersubscribed school, part of an Education Action Zone, with 'serious weaknesses' and a history of behaviour management issues which had been the principle focus for much of their professional development activity for years. They were struggling to find the capacity to engage in enquiry outside of this focus and often resorted to a more traditional INSET approach to address the issue itself. The peer coaches were motivated by the potential that they saw in Thinking Skills to manage behaviour through a combination of social engineering, use of space and kinaesthetic learning. They took the coaching programme back to school as a strategy to tackle a challenge that everyone could recognize and respond to. They were also able to redirect resources from the Education Action Zone (EAZ) and redesignate roles to buy time and support for the programme in school because of the identification of coaching with behaviour management and professional development.

What do leaders of collaborative enquiry and of schools need to do to make sure that enquiry contributes to the overall school development plan?

Are there some areas in which collaborative enquiry can build capacity for improvement where other approaches might not succeed?

2. Context: evaluating the state of readiness of the school and the individual participants. *What do we already know about the focus for the enquiry?*

The network

Immediately identifying a need for more knowledge, the network appointed Dr David Leat from University of Newcastle upon Tyne as a consultant to help them to design an appropriate coaching model to form the focus of their enquiry.

Dr Leat provided a summary of the model that was developed in Newcastle and he outlined their key findings of the model thus far:

- cross-curricular partnerships worked best;
- craft knowledge of the coach must be excellent so it was a good idea to build on existing skills;
- use of video had been the most powerful aspect of the programme;
- an agreement or contract between the partners guaranteeing confidentiality and commitment had been important in establishing ground rules and trust.

The network was thus able to learn both from the research published by the university and from the experiences of another group of schools mediated by the mutual HEI partner.

Taking on board Dr David Leat's suggestion that coaching should build on existing expertise, the network settled on Thinking Skills as the teaching and learning strategy at the heart of their coaching programme and their enquiry. In February 2000, the DfES had launched Best Practice Research Scholarships, in which £2,500 for classroom-based research was made available to teacher–researchers. The network had designed a collaborative enquiry called Thinking Classrooms, in which fourteen of the seventeen network schools participated. As part of the enquiry, teachers from across the curriculum could develop Thinking Skills lessons for their own subjects and evaluate changes in pupil outcomes through document analysis of pupils' work and video evidence of in-class behaviours. They gathered pupil perception data through various feedback mechanisms, including questionnaires. Teacher outcomes were recorded through reflective journals and interviews.

By the end of the year, there was an experience base in most of the schools in the network about what happens when Thinking Skills are introduced into a range of classrooms, with different age ranges and in different subjects. There was also some knowledge and experience of data collection and analysis as part of an enquiry process. In one school in particular, there was considerable knowledge of and interest in coaching through sustained engagement of their science department with the Cognitive Acceleration through Science Education (CASE) methodology (Adey and Shayer 1994), which relies on expert coaching as the mechanism for professional development.

School B – the secondary school

In 1997 the TTA funded four consortia of schools formed to investigate the role of teachers as research and evidence-based practitioners over a three-year period. Each consortium identified their own focus on pupil learning such as inclusion or ICT. School B was in the North East School Based Research Consortium (NESBRC) which comprised a partnership between University of Newcastle upon Tyne, three LEAs and six secondary schools.

The first stage of participation in the TTA consortia project was the development of a pilot project. Lasting about a term it was felt that this would give schools a practice run at enquiry. It would generate a sharp focus to facilitate focused discussion and develop a shared language, an important step in developing the partnership.

This pilot proved invaluable as it provided a vehicle for collaborative lesson and strategy planning and theory development. Engaging with research-provided theory to confirm beliefs about good questioning practice. It was hypothesized that effective use of open questions would encourage longer responses from pupils as well as facilitate greater metacognitive awareness. Engaging in enquiry necessitated data and information gathering. Participants learned about lesson and video observation, which provided excellent CPD – and encouraged newly 'reflective practitioners' to change their practice as a result of evidence revealed to them through video analysis of their lessons and pupil comments gathered through pupil learning logs.

One teacher, for example, was astonished to observe how short and shallow pupils' responses to her questions were when she observed a videoed lesson. When she compared it to the audit of open and closed questions a colleague had recorded for her in the same lesson she was persuaded of a need to investigate her questioning technique further. The qualitative value of both the process and findings of collaborative enquiry were considered to be irrefutable to colleagues who had seldom analysed their own pedagogy in quite so direct a fashion.

The pilot allowed School B to identify learning and development needs, to recruit and motivate even sceptical teachers to participate and to structure their approach to knowledge management.

School A – the primary school

School A invited a colleague who had already worked with the school in various LEA advisory roles and as Regional Director for the Basic Skills Agency to work with the group. She had particular skills which they knew would be useful. Her professional training as an educational psychologist brought a knowledge of child development and pedagogy to the group. The work of the Basic Skills Agency was important in connecting children's learning in school, family and community and in considering innovative approaches to the development of boys' writing.

The school had a history of success and benefited from significant expertise amongst its own team. The headteacher, two 'lead learners', Year 4 and 5 teachers, teaching assistants and representatives from amongst the Foundation Stage, including nursery assistants, were able to contribute a considerable experience and knowledge base to the enquiry.

In each case, this exploration of knowledge and learning needs can be understood by reference to the three fields of knowledge construct introduced in Chapter 1.

Figure 3.1: The three fields of knowledge

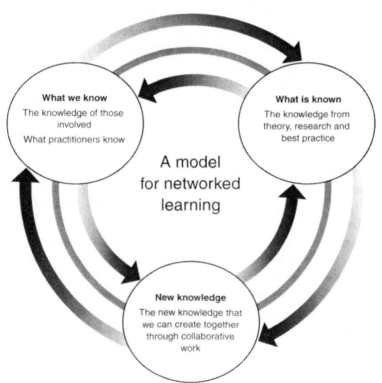

What sources of research and evidence do you believe are most accessible and convincing to practitioners?

Where are the opportunities already in place in your context for practitioners to locate, access and make sense of research and evidence for the development of their practice?

3. Planning: clarifying the content for the enquiry. *What precisely is the question? What's already known 'out there' about it?*

Schools A and B

In the single school examples, there were two different kinds of questions operating at two different levels. The first questions had a pedagogic focus. In School A the focus was on boys' writing, and in School B, it was on teacher questioning techniques. However, in both examples there was another layer of enquiry which was essentially to do with leadership. School A's second enquiry focus was exploring the potential of collaborative enquiry as a development opportunity for middle level leaders. In School B they were engaged in a network-based enquiry investigating teacher research and its use as a methodology for professional development of classroom teachers.

One result of this layering, or nesting, was that the leadership and coordination of the collaborative enquiry became, in both schools, a complex and challenging operation. Crucially it was itself a fundamental part of the learning process. This section addresses specifically the way that enquiry at the first (pedagogic) level was taken forward in the two schools. It then discusses how the formally planned professional development, and the 'informal' professional learning which occurred naturally as part of the work, supported the second (leadership) level. The network example will be dealt with later.

Ownership of the enquiry process was especially important in School A because of the explicit intention to develop leadership capacity in the 'middle' of the school. The school wanted to be in control of its own development. As part of its involvement in networks, the school was committed to participating in six network training days a year. These were the main mechanism for introducing relevant research and practice into the schools in the network. The design of those days built in inter-session tasks, known as 'school-based challenges', for practitioners to undertake back at their school before the next session. The school-based challenges were designed to enable them to test out in practice the theory presented and consider the learning from their discussion of that theory.

The enquiry was managed through development strands that related to key stages. The Foundation/Year 1 strand knew they were trying to answer some profound questions:

- If we say we don't like this jump from Foundation to Year 1 then what do we want it to be like?
- How do you deal with planning?
- How do you deal with coverage when you do things differently and have more play?
- How do we involve families more?
- How do we bridge the gap between home and school learning?

The final question about the gap between home and school learning opened up discussion and debate about the cultural divide educationally. The consultant and the enquiry leader were passionate about the importance of looking to the world outside school as the source for stimulus material for the children, to ensure that the starting points were things that the children would relate to. However not all colleagues were initially convinced about the use of Barbies!

At KS2 the enquiry questions were:

- Can we continue to raise standards without sticking to the literacy hour?
- Can we go back to a themed curriculum?
- Can we think 'outside of the box'?
- If we give children choices will they run away with them?

Differentiation

The schools were at different stages in their development as were the teachers. This had implications for how the learning was led and managed. The work had to be challenging enough for the practitioners with more advanced practice and experience and yet feel 'doable' for less experienced colleagues. In this context the fact that the consultant in School A knew the school and also got to know the practitioners very quickly became a huge advantage.

Best Practice Research Scholarships were another strategy that the school used successfully to maintain the interest of those teachers with more developed practice. Six practitioners in the school held scholarships relating to their enquiry focus.

Who are the change agents in your organization?

What formal and informal networks exist?

Whom do you need to convince in your organization that collaborative enquiry is a useful concept and how might you do that?

4. Operation: leading and managing the enquiry. *Which practitioners and pupils should we work with? Who else needs to be involved? How do we share the outcomes?*

In School B there were a number of strands to the leadership and management of the enquiry. They included appointing a school coordinator, the development of distributed leadership, the use of residential weekends and the development of a coaching model, integrating new members, higher degrees and school-based meetings.

Each of these is discussed in turn in the following sections.

School B – the secondary school

Appointing a school coordinator

Coordinating the collaborative enquiry was a complex leadership task that involved supporting the professional development of colleagues with different levels of confidence and experience in dealing with Thinking Skills, with coaching and with enquiry. It also demanded significant negotiating skills in managing the allocation of resources and in creating a 'space' for the enquiry within the organization. Recruiting to the enquiry and keeping colleagues motivated throughout the rigours of the school year was hard too.

An interesting finding in this and other schools who appoint to this kind of role was the extent to which the coordinator herself experienced professional development even though some were in fact focused on providing learning opportunities for others. The process of supporting collaborative enquiry (or any other form of collaborative CPD for that matter) is itself a learning process in which enquiry becomes the characteristic mode of operation.

The development of distributed leadership

The value of distributed leadership began to emerge in School B as the numbers of staff involved increased. The coordinator was unable to manage all aspects of the work so distributed leadership was a necessary solution.

In School A, distributed leadership was both a purpose for and a focus of the enquiry and provided pivotal learning experiences for practitioners in their roles as lead learners.

Working with headteachers, lead learners from all the primary schools in the network took responsibility for planning a joint training day in their own individual schools. The headteachers agreed that the joint training day in their individual schools would be used as an opportunity to share, with those practitioners not involved in the enquiry, the learning and outcomes from the work so far. The headteachers then decided to 'stand back' and to allow the lead learners to lead.

In School A most of the day involved the lead practitioners presenting the work they had been developing with pupils in their class, and then creating space for staff discussion and questioning. The demonstrations to staff were powerful because they were grounded in practice but with a clear theoretical underpinning. Key Stage 2 staff produced examples of outstanding writing with notes and drafts illustrating the processes and the learning. For one of the lead learners in School A, the day was a complete success and a significant episode of professional development. She felt that it validated the work she had been doing:

> At the end of that day I felt more confident. It made me believe in myself because people were taking on board my ideas. I felt secure. That evening I was going on a train journey to see a friend and I smiled the whole time. It was a lovely feeling.

Use of residential weekends

Residential weekends were an important part of the enquiry process in School B. They offered opportunities for teachers to spend time engaging with the extensive research and evidence underpinning Teaching Thinking. They offered time for reflection – something perceived to be sorely missing from teachers' professional lives – and proved to be an invaluable opportunity for planning and generating ideas. When teachers are able to plan their own Thinking Skills activities they appear to develop a much greater understanding of the metacognitive processes that underpin the Thinking Skills strategies.

The importance of the social dimension at the residential

Teachers meeting together in this informal setting promoted the development of friendship groups. Within these they developed considerable trust, which meant that teachers were more willing to share video footage of lessons that may not have gone as well as they had hoped. This was absolutely essential if they were to help improve each other's practice and understand the processes that contributed to that change.

The implications of numerical growth and change for the residentials

The residential weekend project was designed to be a bottom-up sustainable voluntary initiative. This meant that every year the group was designed to bring on board newcomers and use the initial research and development group to support their development. To facilitate this process a residential weekend was planned for the early part of years two and three of the project.

The first residential weekend of year two of the enquiry had the smallest number of new researchers. The coordinator was concerned that newcomers might feel like outsiders, find it difficult to contribute, and also might have threatened the relationship established by the core group. However that was not the case. This may in part have been as a result of using the core group as 'experts' to support the newcomers. Interestingly, this process appeared to give them confidence when they reflected on just how far they had come in the first year and led the coordinator to realize that they needed to establish this as a strategy for encouraging further progress. In addition, as all teachers recognize, it is often the case that only through having to explain something to someone else does understanding really develop.

Teachers from other schools who were trying to develop Thinking Skills in their own areas were also invited to the residential weekends. Not only was this of benefit to the visitors, it also gave the resident teachers an understanding of their expertise and the importance of their contribution to the research which played a significant part in raising their self-esteem.

Higher degrees

Joint funding of two Masters courses was also invaluable in helping School B to improve expertise in research methodology and allowing it to focus additional research initiatives into the main framework of the school's project. Providing a forum for dissemination of all the research further enhanced the sense of ownership and value felt by those involved.

The network

From each of the seventeen schools participating in the enquiry, three teachers were nominated by the school-based coordinators and authorized

Figure 3.2: The development of the coaching model in the network

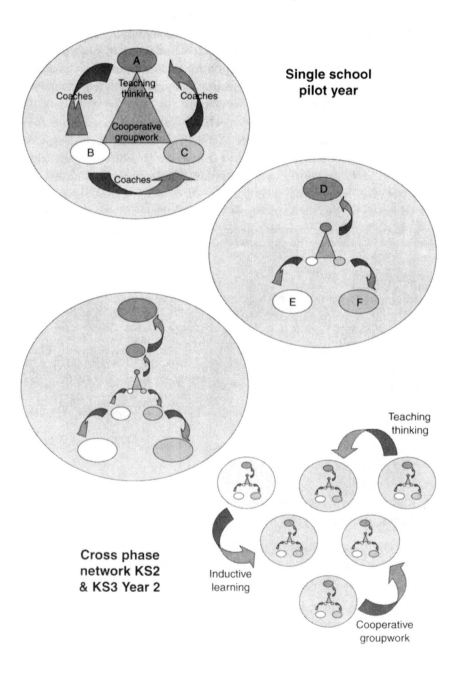

by the headteacher to participate for one year in a pilot programme. The programme required that at least one teacher from each school should be a member of the Senior Leadership Team to ensure that access to release time and cover was as straightforward as possible. It was also important for implementation as the initial practitioners had found through previous activities that this was best achieved by early understanding, ownership and support at a senior level. The programme was structured around six days of development and review seminars throughout the year with the vast majority of work taking place in schools.

The teachers in schools planned a series of meetings throughout the year to review and adjust the research model in real time. Trios designed their own implementation plans and timelines to accommodate the programme and committed to a minimum number of coaching cycles during the year. They would meet again at the beginning of summer term 2002 to evaluate the coaching model and redesign it for presentation at the Annual Conference in June and roll out the following year.

Why coaching?

As coaching is so central to both School B and the network's approaches to collaborative enquiry, it is worth dwelling on the characteristics of coaching to explore why that might be the case.

Coaching can be a powerful tool for professional development. One of its many strengths is that there is a strong element of realism; seeing directly what is going on in the classroom and dealing with it on a personal level. Various models for coaching in schools exist, but they share certain common elements:

- observation;
- demonstration;
- team teaching;
- joining in with the students;
- helping out in the class in a practical way.

Ideally a combination of several of these approaches would be used in a coaching episode. Below are some characteristics of coaching as identified by Dr David Leat (University of Newcastle upon Tyne):

- coaching is a three part process: a pre-lesson discussion which supports planning, an observed lesson and a post-lesson discussion/analysis.
- coaching focuses on teaching skills, teaching styles and lesson episodes – such as questioning, explaining, starters, cooperative group work, peer assessment, teaching thinking, improving motivation.

- a coach is not a universal expert, but someone with expertise in a particular area; peers can coach each other on different issues.
- coaching is a confidential process based on trust.
- the coached teacher does as much of the analysing process as possible so that they are not dependent on the coach indefinitely.
- good coaching has many of the characteristics of conversation – there are episodes and each episode starts at a low cognitive level (describing and explaining) and progresses to a higher cognitive level (hypothesizing and reformulating).
- coaching is often at its most powerful when the people involved teach different subjects.

(Internal network document 2001, pp. 145–6)

One of the distinctive features of coaching is the interdependent learning inherent in the process. Collaboration comes as standard. Coaching also has a focus on detailed and purposeful questioning to inform learning. There is a dataset which forms the subject of the coaching – a video or lesson observation record, pupil feedback or learning outcomes, etc. So in many ways coaching models some of the characteristics of collaborative enquiry but is more time constrained and less open-ended. For all of these reasons, coaching and enquiry are highly compatible and in both School B and the network, coaching was the preferred professional development strategy to support the teachers participating in the enquiry.

Coach as enquirer

While being coached the learning for the coachee is entirely centred on how to teach Thinking Skills better – he/she is not looking for solutions beyond their own classroom. The coach, however, is in enquiry mode. At the same time as enabling the coachee to improve their practice, the coach is making sense of their own practice by analysing the teaching and learning of their coachee as he/she investigates the trends, patterns and anomalies that occur and what practice consistently works or evokes a particular behaviour. Not only does this feedback impact on the coach's own performance, but it enables him/her to make judgements about how best to support teachers in their delivery of Thinking Skills.

If this is the case it may explain why the coordinator's expertise appears never to be exhausted and he/she continues to be able to develop the practice of others. To maximize this learning then it may be better to adapt the model above to ensure that some sort of relationship continues between previous coaches who now coach others. Therefore the learning associated with being a coach becomes another source for enquiry. For example, as one member of staff in School B noted:

When I recall my first coaching experience I am horrified by how unkind I was to the colleague I was coaching. Reflecting on this and comparing responses from the coach and coachee across all those being trained, however, changed how coaching was implemented in the school. Firstly, as Head of Department it had been a mistake to coach a NQT in the same department; there were too many hidden agendas. There was undoubtedly a power relationship at work; secondly, there was a desire to impose my preferred style of teaching the subject; and thirdly, the realization that coaching and mentoring are not the same thing. As a result the group took the decision to coach across departments and to promote coaching which did not involve hierarchical relationships.

In June 2001 the network launched their coaching programme with a two-day residential session.

Day One
Day One focused on the principles and practice of coaching, with lots of opportunities to participate through role-play, demonstration and discussion. Delegates also participated in a Thinking Skills lesson, creating a shared learning opportunity for the whole group which cut across the differences in their curriculum or pedagogic experience before they arrived for the seminar.

Day Two
Day Two was designed to involve participants more closely in some of the detail of the approaches to coaching and Teaching Thinking and to invite them to start thinking about how they would design a coaching programme for themselves within the context of their school.

Participants attended two workshops on the use of video in classrooms. The first focused on the technicalities of optimizing picture and sound quality in poor recording environments (e.g. classrooms) and the second on helping teachers to introduce video into the classroom with minimum disruption for pupils and maximum opportunity for professional development.

Follow-up implementation plans
Before leaving the seminar, each trio was required to complete an implementation plan for the autumn term outlining their commitment and anticipating the support they would require from their school and from the network present to give practical advice and guidance. The plans were photocopied for the programme log and returned to the trio, again to symbolize openness, accountability, active participation and contribution to learning.

Each participant committed to one coaching cycle for the term. That is, each would prepare a Teaching Thinking lesson; meet with their coach to discuss the lesson and the focus for the observation (e.g. lesson start, use of resources, debrief); lead the lesson and have it observed or video recorded, or preferably both; and then hold a plenary session for feedback and planning for the next cycle.

Using video for observation

On the advice of the media team, most teachers decided to experiment with video equipment and try it out in 'safe' lessons first to familiarize themselves with angles and acoustics as well as managing possible changes in the pupils' behaviour with a camera in the room. Observation is sometimes hard to timetable in and is usually the first thing to go when staff are absent. So using video became a capacity-building tactic, which protected the continuity of the programme as well as being a powerful tool for data collection and (self) analysis. The reflections from one teacher about the experience are given below.

Using video for personal/professional development

I had been teaching Thinking Skills for about a year, had tried out a number of activities and was pleased with the results. However, I was becoming frustrated with my own ability to teach Thinking Skills because of the difficulty of the debriefing section of the lesson. The things I wanted to see happen such as lengthy pupil responses, pupil critique and metacognition were not taking place and I couldn't understand what was going wrong.

Living dangerously

A more experienced colleague suggested making a video to see if we could identify the source of the problem. This was a turning point. My colleague was able to identify that the problem lay in my questioning technique; I was asking too many closed or pseudo-open questions. She was also able to suggest changes to the activity, which would encourage more discussion. Introducing cognitive conflict, for instance, meant that not all pupils arrived at the same conclusion.

Impact on lessons

The results of our collaboration were immediately apparent in the next lesson. Rather than having to pressure the pupils in order to elicit a response, I found all my energies being used up trying to ensure that every pupil had a chance to speak! Since then I have compared the two lessons by watching both videos and been amazed at the difference. Without the opportunity of being able to see for myself the effect of my questions, I would not have found it so easy to correct and improve upon my technique for the second attempt. There are some instances where you just have to see the evidence for yourself in order to be convinced.

Skills and confidence

As my skills and confidence in Teaching Thinking have developed, I have taken on the role of coaching others. The coaching programme is based on two cycles: the person being coached observes and videos a Thinking Skills lesson taught by the coach, then s/he teaches their own lesson after discussing what they plan to do with the coach who then observes and videos the lesson. This is discussed and an action plan set out. Both the pre- and post-lesson discussions are videoed in order to help the coach improve their training technique.

The use of video has enabled me to make significant improvements in my own practice and to take a more directive and structured approach to helping coachees adopt new patterns of behaviour.

(Internal network document 2000)

By the time the group met again to review the first term, any initial nervousness about using video had evaporated, to be replaced by a demand for dedicated equipment in each school, such was the pressure on existing resources. The trios had identified a need for using video in other areas of professional development in schools and so they negotiated the purchase of a small video camera for each participating school for the exclusive use of enquiry and CPD initiatives in each school match funded from school funds.

Two further review sessions were held in the north and south of the county in schools from 4.30–6.30 p.m. Twilight sessions were a common feature of the network calendar and in order to accommodate them, travelling time was kept to a minimum, hence the two locations/opportunities. Eight schools attended each session and brought with them video material and resources to share with the group. More importantly, the schools brought their experience, reflections and issues to contribute to discussions about the realities of living out the coaching model in a busy school environment.

School A – the primary school

Keeping the headteacher 'up to speed'

Practitioners engaging in professional development can often end up with more knowledge about a topic than their headteacher. This is not of itself a problem – the headteacher cannot know everything in detail. However, he/she does need to know enough about a development to be able to understand its implications for their own school. Headteacher support was crucial to the success of a school's enquiry strategy. Headteachers did attend the training when they could, but when this was not possible, the practitioners in the enquiry organized headteacher briefing sessions to ensure that headteachers would understand why they were trying to implement certain activities as a result of what they were learning.

Headteachers were then more likely to be supportive. Part of the practitioners' solution to the difficulty of keeping headteachers informed and 'up to speed' was to hold a network training day in the summer term. A summary of the Networked Learning Community training day of which School A was a part is given below.

The summer term network training day took place at a large hotel, involved all headteachers and practitioners from the schools and was organized as a 'World Café', a collaborative enquiry structured over a limited period of time that optimized knowledge transfer between different groups of practitioners. It was designed to be an opportunity for practitioners, and headteachers in particular, to take an active part in developing their understanding of the work of all the schools in addition to their own.

There were two days – one for KS1 and one for KS2. Headteachers were asked to attend both days, so they could understand and absorb progress in both key stages and understand the implications for their own school.

The process

1 Every school set up their 'stall' to display their learning.
2 Each headteacher was invited to work with a group of teachers that were not from their own school. The lead learners and teachers were encouraged to explain their work to the group.
3 The headteachers and lead learners then stayed at their stall responding to questions and encouraging discussion with visiting groups while the rest of the school's staff moved to another group.
4 Groups moved round four times, enabling as much 'sharing' of ideas as possible.
5 Time was allocated for all headteachers and staff to wander freely and make connections with other schools, share ideas, etc.

When the 'carousel' was complete the headteachers came together for a structured discussion about the work that led into a formal evaluation of the first year of the network's learning.

What strategies could you use to make time and money available to support collaborative enquiry in your school or organization?

Which groups of practitioners would benefit/contribute most to collaborative enquiry in your school or organization?

How can everyone be kept informed and involved?

5. Sustainability: managing implementation and change resulting from the outcomes of the enquiry. *What will happen next?*

School B developed an approach to sustainability that combined the celebratory and motivational atmosphere of large group gatherings with the deeper and more trusting relationships and interdependences built over time in small group arrangements. The schools identified a need to provide opportunities for discussion of professional findings, the progress being made and the implications for the future, which generated significant enthusiasm amongst participants. Teacher researchers found these large group opportunities extremely motivating and reported significant changes in practice as a result.

But although these larger sessions offered an opportunity for ideas generation it was only in small groups that long-lasting sustainable change took place. The relationships built through the coaching partnerships and through the residentials proved to be the most enduring and fostered the most significant changes to practice. Collaboration in a sustained partnership develops features of friendship, trust, mutuality, confidentiality and history. Designing opportunities for teachers to generate professional relationships based around work and learning that share these characteristics was powerful and affecting for participants.

> 'I have experienced every conceivable form of INSET in my 25 years of teaching experience. It took nearly a year for me to video my teaching, a few months before I watched it myself and almost another year before I allowed anyone else to watch it. Coaching and especially videoing had a more profound impact on my teaching than any other CPD activity I have been involved in.'

The bottom-up small-scale approach proved to be highly sustainable and, for School B, explains how sociability encouraged significant leaps forward in thinking and practice.

> '… we have completely changed our approach to teaching and there are at least two of us who are adamant that we would not be still teaching if we had not had such a stimulating strand to our career development.'

A model for sustainability

The experience of School B advocates an alternative model of adult learning from the more traditional delivery mode and the school developed a significant theoretical approach to articulate their thinking. Figure 3.3 demonstrates an enquiry-based approach to the application of a Teaching

Figure 3.3: The 'Waves of involvement' model developed at School B

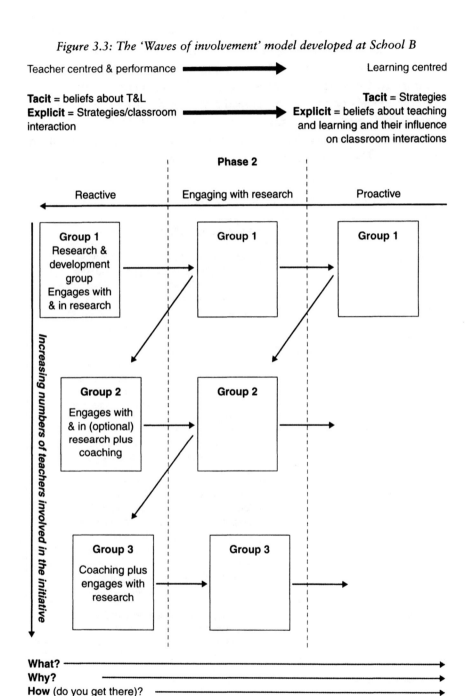

Thinking strategy. W. W. Rostow, an economist interested in understanding the economic development of countries, developed the Model of Economic Development which suggests that countries pass through a number of stages as they progress to economic maturity.

Informed by Rostow's theory, the school coordinator, with support from the university partner, developed a way of describing their school's research and development group, its engagement with Teaching Thinking and the subsequent involvement of other classroom practitioners in its application. They call this the 'Waves of involvement' model (see p. 95).

Model of development of Teaching Thinking through enquiry

	Example of activity/practice
Reactively engaging with research	Being provided with some theoretical input at a residential or being provided with some topical reading material. Highlights the importance of effective facilitation and knowledge of stages of development of individual or groups of enquirers.
Proactively engaging with research	Having generated questions about their practice teachers endeavour to find explanations. Searching helpful websites such as GTCE Research of the Month or searching professional journals were common examples.
Engaging with and in research	Teachers actually doing it for themselves. Videoing, analysing and coding videos, for example.
Teacher centred	Initially this was thought to be the teacher focused primarily on themselves. In the early stages of video analysis, for example, almost every teacher watching themselves on tape comments on hair, build, voice or something similar. Over time the comments become a little more sophisticated and start to focus on their behaviours, commands, questions, etc.
Learner centred	This appeared to be where the person observing the video would focus on pupil questions or interactions, for example, as well as on evidence of what and how pupils were learning.

What does this tell us about leading collaborative enquiry in schools?

One debate around Rostow's model discusses the need for a country to pass through each stage of development in its drive to maturity. When we use the model to analyse participation in enquiry, it raises an interesting question for planning and operation of collaborative enquiry in schools. Does everyone need to start at the beginning and go through all the stages or can some benefit from the previous learning of others?

If a school wishes to trial a range of different learning theories, the development of a number of different research and development groups, connected by a school improvement strategy, to pilot and enquire can be a powerful recipe for ensuring staff commitment and competence.

Movement between the developmental phases appears to be associated with the mode of questioning the teachers engaged in. Initially teachers focused on what was happening in the classroom and what they were doing that impacted on classroom performance. Over the months that followed teachers engaged with the reasons for these processes, asking 'why' before investigating 'how' they could adapt pupil and teacher behaviour for maximum benefit.

Sustaining coaching as enquiry in the network: the appointment of a Key Stage 3 consultant

The solution to sustaining enquiry through coaching in the network was creative and opportunistic and indicative of the strength of commitment within the participating schools. One of the original forty-eight teachers was appointed to become a Key Stage 3 consultant. He maintained a firm commitment throughout the application and selection process to the value of coaching as an approach to knowledge and practice transfer that could support the implementation of national strategies. Clearly the selection panel agreed and immediately after his appointment, the consultant began negotiations with the network research officer and the team leader for KS3 to adapt the coaching model for use in KS3. This of course meant that time and funding became available to support the further development of coaching within the network.

Called the KS3 Peer Coaching Model for Teachers (see p. 99), the new programme preserved three key aspects from the original network coaching programme design:

- the commitment to cross-curricular groupings;
- the promotion and support for the use of video for evidence gathering and reflection;

- the dynamic and potential for sustainability of the non-hierarchical, cross-curricular trio was still deemed the most appropriate formation.

In addition, several significant and exciting changes were made to redesign the model for KS3:

- *The identification of a learning focus*
  Assessment for Learning was introduced alongside Thinking Skills, as another teaching strategy developed through KS3.

- *The expansion of the constituency*
  Formerly an upper school only model, the new programme also recruited from middle schools. In a three-tier system, KS3 is split across two schools and liaison therefore becomes enormously important. In some cases trios were constituted from different schools and different phases. Collaborative learning opportunities across the phases became a major opportunity to strengthen understandings and improve professional relationships.

Guidance from local 'experts'

The expert input came from the local KS3 consultants drawing on their training and experience of working as part of the KS3 team. Access to resources, venues and the profile of a national strategy pushed coaching up the agenda for participating schools. The 'additional support' to schools was used to support clusters of schools in the network who were brought together to share learning in ways that were mutually supportive and likely to help schools address the achievement gaps between pupils. The experience of teachers who were participants in the 'pilot' was also employed explicitly (e.g. as presenters at events) and implicitly through continued involvement in the new model.

A clearly articulated plan

In contrast to the discovery or action enquiry model of the first year, participants had the security of a scaffolded programme to help them manage their learning. Collaborative enquiry at the school level was, however, clearly evident in both the structure and space for adaptation and exploration in the design.

The KS3 Peer Coaching Model

Stage 1: Establish trios

> It is best if teachers are from different subject areas and from different schools. The trios are non-hierarchical.

Stage 2: Knowledge acquisition

> It is important that teachers have the opportunity to learn too! Through active learning sessions, teachers are introduced to a wide variety of thinking skills approaches and also to the key aspects of assessment for learning.

Stage 3: Find a focus

> Teachers choose a teaching strategy or approach with which they are unfamiliar, but which could be used to deliver the teaching topic they have in their schemes of work. Teachers should not rewrite what they usually do ... just do it differently! It is best if all three teachers can work on the same strategy or approach. It is also important to choose a strategy or approach which suits the learning intentions of the lesson.

Stage 4: Planning

> Teachers meet and plan the three lessons. They generate the materials they need to support the lesson and agree times when the lesson will be delivered. In an ideal world, the planning session should be videoed.

Stage 5: Lesson

> The lessons are delivered, observed and videoed. Usually, one member of the coaching trio observes the lessons and the pattern is as follows: Teacher A observes Teacher B; Teacher B observes Teacher C; Teacher C observes Teacher A.

Stage 6: Reflection

> One-to-one feedback takes place and it is best to focus on at least two successful aspects of the lesson and one aspect for development. There should then be a final feedback session involving all members of the trio.

('The Art of Coaching', internal network document 2002)

Whilst there is no doubt that the coaching model will continue to adapt to changing priorities, personnel and participants, in its third year at the time of writing, it appears robust, well supported and with a healthy recruitment. From a radical, small-scale and experimental design, coaching evolved into a systemic solution to implementation of a national strategy and was considered to be part of the professional learning entitlement of teachers in this network. With collaborative enquiry at its heart, it honoured the core values of the network and became a way of making sense of external initiatives in the context of a commitment to networked learning.

School A – the primary school

The key to sustaining collaborative enquiry in the primary school has been the extent to which it has visibly impacted on learning outcomes for both teachers and pupils. Ultimately, what will persuade teachers to participate (and to participate again) is the sense that they are making a difference to the children in their classrooms.

Below, three teachers from School A share their experiences of participating in collaborative enquiry and the effect it has had on themselves and their pupils:

Debbie's story: innovation and achievement

Debbie, a Year 6 teacher, was appointed as a 'lead learner' in the collaborative enquiry because she was the leading literacy teacher and was being 'fired up' by her new learning via a Best Practice Research Scholarship (BPRS). Debbie is quite clear about the impact of the experience: 'doors started to open for me and I was getting excited about the learning for me and for my children.'

For Debbie the enquiry experience brought together some key elements of her previous professional learning which had involved the development of emotional intelligence, and a BPRS investigating the affect of Brain Gym and brain-based learning theories on achievement at KS2.

The experience of being part of an enquiry network opened up for Debbie other ways of approaching the design of the learning in her classroom. As she observed: 'I felt that I had been on tram lines for the past three years since I started teaching and the project helped me move from them and take risks. I was given the freedom to try new things, even with my Year 6 class.'

Debbie and her headteacher agreed at the beginning of Year 6, the first year of the project, that they would not mention SATs to the Year 6 children until after Easter and that then they would just show them and go over one or two papers to familiarize them. The headteacher crossed her fingers, held her breath and trusted that 'good practice will out'.

A visitor to Debbie's class would have seen some children learning at the inter-active whiteboard, some learning individually, some engaged in their learning tasks on the floor and some boys in the Year 6 class would be learning in the role-play corner which had been set up as an office! This latter development of setting up the role-play corner as an office proved to be a powerful strategy for supporting boys' literacy. Some boys even decided to stay in at playtime to 'work' in the office.

The Year 6 SATs results particularly in writing were the best ever, with 94 per cent of children achieving Level 4 and an astonishing 62 per cent of those achieving Level 5.

Kate's story: risk and leadership

Kate, a Year 6 teacher, is clear that the collaborative enquiry 'allowed me to explore ideas' and 'gave me the flexibility and freedom I needed'. Through her participation, Kate was able to link development work on Emotional Intelligence (EI) with work on literacy at KS2. Empathy had been one of the priorities in the development of the EI work, to help pupils understand how to express themselves and to explore their own and others' emotions. The project gave the children a vocabulary they could use when empathizing with characters in their reading and writing.

Kate says that 'you have to be brave to let go of traditional approaches'. Her planning and design of the literacy hour became much more fluid as a result of the enquiry. She and other teachers learned how to use art, and more particularly, film as a strategy to improve literacy. Kate and her headteacher believe that her use of film was a major breakthrough with her class and inspired the children to produce some outstanding written work. She has since extended the approach to encourage children to draw their thoughts and responses together before starting to write them.

Her developments helped particularly with the boys' understanding of personifi-cation. The 'connectivity' with the development of the work on EI has had a powerful impact. Working with children to develop their EI meant that they were able to develop their own vocabulary to describe and understand their own emotions and to use that vocabulary to enhance their writing. There is evidence of the children trans-ferring their learning in emotional literacy into their writing.

Kate has since taken on responsibility for leading the work on emotional literacy in the school.

Lewis' story: motivation for pupils ... and the teacher

Lewis, a teacher in his third year of teaching was the ICT coordinator for the school and with his own class in Year 5. The focus for his enquiry was how to exploit the use of ICT as a motivating tool for boys to support their literacy development and in particular their writing.

Lewis learned that giving a context that boys can relate to and a 'real-life' flavour to the learning was a key motivator for the boys in their writing. Lewis was able to use his ICT skills to support a report writing assignment that was based around delivering the news. The assignment took two weeks and the boys did not begin to write their report until very near the end of the time.

The planning for the report was where much of the learning took place as the boys analysed news reports on TV, and focused in particular on the techniques that the news presenters used, for example how to form a 'link' between one item and the next. This involved the use of a range of equipment – digital video cameras, interactive whiteboards, laptops and the Internet. Again it was the time given to the research that helped the pupils develop the vocabulary and speaking and listening skills they needed.

The end of the topic involved all pupils actually doing the news filming and presenting their own televised news bulletin. Lewis is in no doubt about the impact of the experience on his classroom practice: 'I felt like I was seeing things for the first time. It was the first time I had experienced proper training. It was the first time I had a proper scaffolding for understanding how to teach the boys writing.'

Conclusion

In this chapter we have considered the following elements of the practice of collaborative enquiry. They are summarized below:

Purpose: identifying the issue to be addressed
- Collaborative enquiry takes hold and has impact when its purposes support the overall development needs of the school.
- Finding ways of connecting collaborative enquiry with other initiatives helps to make sense of lots of different kinds of activities.

Context: evaluating the state of readiness of the school and the individual participants
- It is very important to identify the right people to lead and to participate in the enquiry; they may not always be the most senior or experienced practitioners in the school.
- Collaborative enquiry needs to connect with research and evidence outside of school. The LEA, local HEI or a national organization may be good partners in this.

Planning: clarifying the content for the enquiry
- A good enquiry focus is small enough to make sense to an individual pupil or practitioner and generalizable enough to find a wider audience for its outcomes.
- Good evidence from pupils' work and improved outcomes will get practitioners' attention.

Operation: leading and managing the enquiry

- Leading collaborative enquiry is hard work but worth it.
- There is significant professional development in taking on a leadership or coordination role in school.
- Negotiating resources, especially time for participation, is a skilled logistical and political activity. The support, but not necessarily the direct involvement, of headteachers is crucial.
- Developing a variety of enquiry processes, including videoing, coaching, formal inputs, residentials and a range of informal opportunities.

Sustainability: managing implementation and change resulting from the outcomes of the enquiry

- Lots of things happen when collaborative enquiry takes off in schools. It becomes the energy and information source for change and improvement. It is also itself constantly adapting and changing to the new environment that it contributes so much to creating.
- Ultimately what will influence continuous participation is evidence that collaborative enquiry has a positive impact for children.

References

Adey, P. and Shayer, M. (1994) *Really Raising Standards: Cognitive Intervention and Academic Achievement*, London: Routledge.

Previewing Chapter 4

We conclude Chapter 3 in exactly the right place; with the difference that collaborative enquiry can make for pupils. Mostly that difference can be seen and felt in the changes to practice that result from the processes and the outcomes of enquiry. So for instance, as teachers learn to collaborate in new and purposeful ways, they begin to model those skills for their pupils. An increase in the incidence of teacher collaboration is almost always mirrored by an increase in pupil collaboration. Another effect that collaborative enquiry has for practitioners and pupils is that it generates confidence to take risks in teaching and learning and as classrooms become more exciting places, motivation increases for everyone in them.

But there are subtler and deeper changes that begin to take shape. Practitioners who engage in enquiry have different conversations with their pupils from those who don't. They ask different kinds of questions, which challenge the children intellectually of course, but they also begin to change the relationship between teacher and pupil.

This is the beginning of a process that actively engages pupils in collaborative enquiry in school. In the next chapter, Michael Fielding and Sara Bragg show us just how far that process can take us. They provide a rationale for including students in enquiry as researchers, discuss the different types of involvement and provide concrete examples of students as researchers in both primary and secondary settings. The second part of the chapter offers practical advice for colleagues in schools about how to actually manage the process of students as researchers.

4 It's an equal thing ... It's about achieving together: student voices and the possibility of a radical collegiality

Sara Bragg and Michael Fielding

Collaborative enquiry can be a democratizing process in a school. It involves sharing and distributing leadership and encouraging all members of the school to be active 'enquirers' into the life and work of the school. This includes students. Without the involvement of the students it is not possible to enquire effectively either into the learning and teaching processes or into the school itself.

Sara Bragg and Michael Fielding build from the work that they have been doing in the field of Students as Researchers to make the case for students to have a central role in the enquiry process in school. The rationale for this, given in this chapter, is based upon a different set of assumptions about the nature of education and the role of 'schooling' in the twenty-first century and a different and developing understanding of what it means to be a teacher or a student.

The chapter seeks to answer the following questions:

1 Why involve young people in collaborative enquiry?
2 What are the different types of student engagement as researchers?
3 What examples are there of student enquiry in action?
4 What are the benefits of student enquiry?
5 How do you start and sustain student enquiry?
6 What dilemmas and issues are posed by the development of Students as Researchers?

1. Why involve young people in collaborative enquiry?

This section outlines the reasons for including students in collaborative enquiry. It includes a discussion of:

- a shift to working with students collegially rather than collaboratively;

- discussion of issues of agency and autonomy of students;
- changes in the boundaries between students and teachers.

Elsewhere in this book, contributors argue that enquiry has many benefits for teachers and schools. Here, we argue that students should be involved in collaborative enquiry too. This is a different argument because it presumes a different logic and set of assumptions about the nature of education and the place of formal schooling within it. It is a stronger argument because it suggests we need to re-examine both what it means to be a teacher and what it means to be a student. In other words we hold that student involvement in enquiry with teachers, not merely 'collaboratively', but sometimes 'collegially', holds out the possibility of a bridge to quite different forms of schooling in the new millennium.

One familiar rationale for student involvement in enquiry was captured by one of our student researcher interviewees who suggested that 'education is for students and therefore students should have a say in it'. This is an argument about agency and autonomy – students being able to change or influence what goes on in schools – that is central to what is meant by education. It stands in stark contrast to recent research which suggests that in practice schools still provide disappointingly few opportunities for students to contribute meaningfully to shaping school life (Alderson and Arnold 1999; Wyse 2001).

Arguments about agency and autonomy are also strengthened by concerns about social justice. In recent years young people in schools have come under increasing pressure, including a more persistent burden of testing and heavy scrutiny of their performance. To deny them any voice in debating the wisdom or effectiveness of such arrangements would seem to undermine the deeper rationale of the testing itself, namely to produce a more alert and capable workforce and a more engaged and responsible citizenry. Certainly, there is evidence that current education policy is moving towards greater student consultation and involvement. For instance, the 2002 Education Act now requires schools to consult with pupils, whilst Ofsted expects inspectors to report on how far a school 'seeks, values and acts on pupils' views'.

More broadly, we hold that the old certainties about the boundaries between teacher and student are starting to change. In the light of these changes, involving students in the processes of collaborative enquiry is more desirable and more promising for all parties than it has been for a considerable time.

Of course, this is not universally the case and there are many interesting and important examples of imaginative and committed practice that are much more cautious and prescribed in their feel and intentions.

This chapter explores how teachers and young people have worked together on collaborative enquiry in schools, taking one approach – Students as Researchers – that has developed in the UK in the last ten years (Crane 2001; Fielding 1998, 1999, 2001a,b,c; Fielding and Bragg 2003; Fielding and Prieto 2000; Harding 2001; Kirby 1999, 2001; Prieto 2001; Raymond 2001; Wetherill 1998; Worrall *et al.* 1999) and has many companion projects operating across the world (Holdsworth 2000a and b; Levin 1998, 2000a and b; Lincoln 1995; Mitra 2001; Oldfather 1995; Silva 2001; Steinberg and Kincheloe 1998).

2. What are the different types of student engagement as researchers?

Student involvement ranges along a continuum. This sections distinguishes the different modes of students as researchers. These include:

- students as data source;
- students as active respondents;
- students as co-researchers;
- students as researchers.

Students as Data Source

Teacher role	Acknowledge + use information about student performance
Student role	Receive a better-informed pedagogy
Teacher engagement with students	Dissemination
Classroom e.g.	Data about student past performance
Team/Dept e.g.	Looking at samples of students' work
School e.g.	Student attitude surveys, cohort-based exam + test scores

With 'Students as Data Source' there is a real teacher commitment to pay attention to the student voice speaking through the practical realities of work done and targets agreed. It acknowledges that for teaching and learning to improve there is a need to take more explicit account of relevant data about individual students and group or class performance. Students are thus recipients of a better informed pedagogy. Teachers are helped to understand more about students through the effective dissemination of information about their performance or attitudes. At classroom level 'Students as Data Source' expresses itself through things like data about student past performance. At team or department level it might involve looking at samples of students' work, whilst at whole school level it might take the form of student attitude surveys and cohort-based exam and test results.

Students as Active Respondents

Teacher role	Hear what students say
Student role	Discuss their learning + approaches to teaching
Teacher engagement with students	Discussion
Classroom e.g.	Shared lesson objectives/explicit assessment criteria
Team/Dept e.g.	Students evaluate a unit of work
School e.g.	Traditional school council/peer-led action groups

With 'Students as Active Respondents' there is a teacher willingness to move beyond the accumulation of passive data and a desire to hear what students have to say about their own experience in lessons and in school. Students are thus discussants rather than recipients of current approaches to teaching and learning. Dissemination of existing information is supplemented and transcended through the teacher's commitment to make meaning out of that data through active discussion with his/her students.

At the classroom level this might express itself through the negotiation of lesson objectives or learning intentions and the nuanced and attentive exchanges typical of good assessment for learning practices. At the team or department level this might involve students in the evaluation of units or schemes of work. At whole-school level it might express itself through traditional school councils that respond to existing systems and arrangements within the school or by the establishment of peer-led action groups on issues such as drugs, sexuality and counselling.

Students as Co-researchers

Teacher role	Listen in order to learn
Student role	Co-researcher with teacher on agreed issues
Teacher engagement with students	Dialogue (teacher-led)
Classroom e.g.	Focus groups conducted by student co-researchers
Team/Dept e.g.	Students assist in team/dept action research
School e.g.	Transition between primary/secondary school

'Students as Co-researchers' sees an increase in both student and teacher involvement, and more partnership than the two previous types. Whilst student and teacher roles are not equal, they are moving more strongly in an egalitarian direction. Students move from being discussants to being co-researchers into matters of agreed significance and importance. Whilst the boundaries of action and exploration are fixed by the teacher, and whilst he/she typically identifies (again usually through negotiation) what it is that is to be investigated, explored and better understood, the commitment and agreement of students is essential. This change in relationship is matched by a change in the form and manner of teacher engagement with students: hearing is supplemented by the more attentive listening. Since there is a much richer and more overt interdependence in the 'Student as Co-researcher' mode, discussion is replaced by teacher-led dialogue. Teacher and students are in a much more exploratory mode.

At the classroom level this might express itself through the teachers' desire to extend their pedagogy and begin to take more risks even though, or perhaps especially because, the class is proving difficult and unresponsive. Student-led focus groups are one example of this co-researcher approach which produced substantial improvements for the teacher and students of a Year 9 Modern Foreign Language class. At the team or department level 'Student as Co-researchers' work might involve students helping teachers to design and carry out research into why Year 9 girls seemed disenchanted with some aspects of the subject, or, in a primary-school context, how greater independence in learning might be encouraged at KS1. At whole-school level it might express itself through joint research into issues of transition between primary and secondary school or between different Key Stages within a school.

Students as Researchers

Teacher role	Listen in order to contribute
Student role	Initiator and director of research with teacher support
Teacher engagement with students	Dialogue (student-led)
Classroom e.g.	What makes a good lesson?
Team/Dept e.g.	Gender issues in technology subjects
School e.g.	Evaluation of e.g. PSHE system, radical school council

Our fourth type – 'Students as Researchers' – (Fielding 1998, 2001b) deepens and extends the egalitarian thrust we noted with 'Students as Co-researchers'. Partnership remains the dominant working motif, but here it is the voice of the student that comes to the fore and in a leadership or initiating, not just a responsive, role. It is students who identify issues to be researched and who undertake the research with the support of teachers. They have responsibility for making sense of the data, writing a report or presenting their findings; and it is students to whom the class teacher, team, department or school community are bound to respond in ways which are respectful, attentive and committed to positive change. Dialogue is at the heart of this mode of working. The dialogue is student led rather than teacher led and, potentially at any rate, the exploratory impetus of 'Students as Co-researchers' is further enhanced by the pivotal place of student perceptions and perspectives in the conduct of the research.

At the classroom level 'Students as Researchers' have typically engaged with topics such as 'What makes a good lesson?', the possible link between classroom seating arrangements and student behaviour and factors that help and hinder learning. At the team or department level Student as Researcher work has investigated matters like the apparent gender divide in technology subjects, the effectiveness of homework and the tutorial programme. At whole-school level students have researched the effectiveness or otherwise of rewards systems, bullying and harassment, ITT arrangements, an entire PSHE system and the development of new playground facilities.

How has your thinking been stimulated by these models of student involvement?

3. What examples are there of student enquiry in action?

Students as Researchers believes that young people and adults often have quite different views of what is significant or important in their experience of and hopes for learning, and that even when they identify similar issues as important, they can understand quite different things by them. The starting point is students' questions (as well as, or even instead of, teachers' questions) and, if students are given support to enable them to pursue their enquiries, we often find that new knowledge emerges about learning, about teaching and about ourselves as teachers and learners. For this process to be productive and engaging, we need to create conditions of dialogue in which we listen to and learn from each other in new ways for new purposes.

Students as Researchers promotes partnerships in which students work alongside teachers to mobilize their knowledge of school and become 'change agents' of its culture and norms. It seeks to develop amongst students and teachers a sense of shared responsibility for the quality and conditions of teaching and learning, both within particular classrooms and more generally within the school as a learning community. In the projects described below, specific groups of students identify and investigate issues related to their schools and their learning that they see as significant. The projects aim to enable students to work with teachers in bringing about change, or even to take the lead, with teachers supporting and facilitating the process. Students as Researchers seeks to involve, not merely to use, young people, viewing them not just as recipients or targets, but as resources and producers of knowledge.

This section provides examples of student enquiry in action. This includes:

- individual teachers working with students;
- several enquiry groups;
- researching teaching and learning;
- the work of the School Council;
- changing school structures and processes.

Individual teachers working with students

As our earlier typology of student-voice work suggested, Students as Researchers can be approached at the level of the individual teacher, the team or department or the whole school or college. For instance, an individual teacher might wish to develop greater participation within his/ her own practice. This may be a way to test the climate and build confidence before developing more widespread initiatives, and it can happen whether or not the school culture supports it. In such cases, a Students as Researchers project might involve a short-term or one-off enquiry, a series of groups recruited one after another or one teacher sustaining one student enquiry group over a longer period, gradually enabling it to take on a wider range of tasks.

Several enquiry groups

Student enquiry projects might also involve several teachers and several groups – for instance, team/department members can consult students about how their joint work might be better developed, in terms of the content, the teaching approach or assessment processes. A commitment to student voice and to accessing students' views through student-led research might also be built into school policy. Here Students as Researchers might involve a number of student research groups, some of whom are experienced and some newer, various teachers, some older students supporting each group and an overall coordinator. In both the latter cases, a greater degree of senior staff involvement and support is necessary.

The number of Students as Researchers groups running at any one time need not necessarily be limited. One school, for instance, worked with 30 students from each of Years 7, 8 and 9, each organized into smaller sub-groups of about six students. Appointing an overall coordinator can help to make links between the teams, liaise between staff and students, enable groups to learn from each other and ensure that they are aware of what is happening in other groups.

Researching teaching and learning

In the schools with whom we have worked, students have researched issues to do with teaching and learning such as: what makes a good teacher?; what makes a good lesson?; what helps and hinders learning?; and drop-out in particular subjects. They have explored school and curriculum policy on issues such as: pastoral programmes and PSHE; careers awareness and guidance; profiling and assessment; GCSE or post-16 choices; induction into the sixth form; bullying policies and truanting. They have investigated school organization and environment such as: playground layout and design; use of footballs in the playground; dining-room arrangements such as queuing; 'safe and unsafe places' within the school grounds; refurbishing toilets and social areas.

In one secondary school, for example, teachers selected as researchers eighteen students (nine boys and nine girls) from Year 8, which the school had identified as a 'lost' year that sometimes failed to reach its full potential. A presentation at a year assembly showed their commitment and hard work on behalf of others and seemed to help overcome the resentment that some other students had initially felt at not being included. The students produced three reports and Powerpoint presentations. The research into 'What makes a good lesson', for example, emphasized teachers' and students' shared perspectives, and students' role in successful learning. Teachers recognized that they had underestimated Year 8 – that 'students as the 'receivers' of our teaching are an underused resource', as the deputy head put it. They became more receptive to student input into curriculum planning. The KS3 coordinator observed a positive impact, particularly on the learning of other Year 8 boys. She commented that the student researchers 'take the skills they've learned back into their lessons. It rubs off on other students, and it rubs out the "boff" thing, so it takes the lid off to allow the development of the whole year'.

The work of the School Council

In a primary school, members of the school's active and popular School Council investigated children's perceptions of the effectiveness of the school's buddy system. The research began in February and the final report was completed in June. Children chose to conduct playground observations (contrasting days when buddies were present and when they were not), to run focus groups, to email other schools to find out how their buddy system worked and if it was a success and to write a questionnaire. Groups of five to six children each took responsibility for one of these areas and results were discussed in subsequent School Council meetings. The report itself revealed interesting divergences of opinion: for instance, whilst younger children in the school were supportive of the system, older boys in particular seemed to have negative attitudes towards it. The School Council discussed why this might be and what might be done about it. The researchers were also highly reflective about the advantages and disadvantages of each of the approaches they had chosen, and had clearly learnt a great deal about enquiry methods (for further details, see Hannam, forthcoming).

Changing school structures and processes

Students' input, based on their own research evidence, can make a significant contribution to changing school structures and processes. One example is a research project into the use of trainee (ITT) teachers within the school. Students from Years 10–12 carried out focus group discussions and individual interviews with other students and wrote a report noting inconsistencies in the use of trainee teachers across different departments. They proposed a means by which students could work with trainee teachers to establish dialogues about teaching and learning. Eventually teacher-training practices were significantly reorganized as a result of the recommendations and the initiative became an accepted, and voluntary, part of trainee teachers' experience in the school. One trainee teacher stated that student feedback 'has often been the most helpful professional training I have had in my first year of teaching'. Students noted that their participation gave them new insights into teaching. Moreover, permanent teachers became interested and started to include student feedback as part of their normal way of working.

Finally, a school identified teaching and learning in the sixth form as one of its priority areas for school improvement, noting particular problems to do with the transition from GCSE to post-16 study. One member of staff was given a responsibility point to recruit and support a group of twelve students whose brief was to help the school understand student perspectives on the issue. The process lasted from November to the summer term. Students met weekly at lunchtimes. They carried out lesson observations, then designed a questionnaire for students, asking them about their preferred teaching approaches, areas where they felt they lacked skills, the characteristics of good teachers and good students and students' use of time. The data collected emphasized students' responsibilities in contributing to successful learning and teaching. Through the enquiry, students were able to communicate their need for help, for instance with organizing files and folders, or their preferences – such as for having homework set in the middle rather than at the end of lessons. The researchers used their findings to design postcards. One side of each postcard contained a written finding; on the other side was a witty cartoon (drawn by students) that made the same point. The postcards provided a talking point amongst teachers and students and teachers often referred to them in lessons. Students commented that they felt that teachers were indeed listening to their concerns, and this had helped improve staff–student relationships.

Which of the examples given has most relevance for your school's current stage of development?

What benefits could you see accruing in your own school by the development of Students as Researchers?

4. What are the benefits of student enquiry?

Our evidence suggests that Students as Researchers projects can have a positive impact on students, teachers, and their schools. This section discusses:

- the benefit for students, in particular increased motivation and creativity as well as generic skill development;
- the benefits for teachers, in particular the development of more positive and productive relationships with students and the improvement of learning and teaching;
- the benefits for schools, in particular the impact on school culture and school improvement.

Benefits for students

The development of motivation and creativity

Student researchers described the pleasures of participating in purposeful activities addressing issues that they define as important, that are challenging and have an impact or consequence which extends beyond the participants. They often realize that they are capable of more than they thought and that they can develop a perspective and point of view (for instance, through writing recommendations for action). Knowing that students' views are having an impact on how things are done in the school and classroom gives satisfaction and pride. At the same time, however, the research reports are not formally assessed, and (in most cases) a sympathetic member of staff supports students in their work. This combination of factors means that students can be exploratory and take risks. It might explain the creativity and commitment students bring to the process, which has been particularly evident in their determination to develop approaches that will involve a wider range of students and to communicate their research to others, often in striking and attention-grabbing ways.

In Students as Researchers projects, students experience a more flexible learning structure and environment than is typical of most school lessons – one in which they have considerable control over what they do. This often generates excitement and commitment. Students repeatedly comment on how much they enjoy self-motivated activity, where they have greater choice over the pace and style of approach and opportunities for planning, acting and reflecting.

Supporting generic skill development

In the process of planning and doing the research, student researchers learn useful new skills – in a context where they are relevant and meaningful.

For instance, they acquire academic skills that are helpful in future study and work. These include identifying research questions; devising schedules for questionnaires, interviews or observations; conducting interviews or focus groups with both adults and peers; analysing and interrogating public documents; data interpretation; writing for different contexts (e.g. reports and newsletters); and using relevant software packages for analysing and presenting data such as Excel or Powerpoint. They acquire communication and presentation skills and become more confident communicators because they are required to speak in public to different audiences. They also develop 'civic' skills such as those of running meetings, drawing up agenda, taking minutes, chairing and turn-taking.

In Students as Researchers projects, students experience new ways of collaborating with and learning from each other and teachers. The process of conducting a research project usually involves working in teams for an extended period and developing the range of skills that effective team work requires.

Student researchers often form new bonds with teachers and come to perceive teachers differently by working with them in a different way. They often comment that they now know 'how difficult it is for teachers to teach!' and recognize that successful teaching and learning involves mutual responsibilities, remarking, for instance: 'I am aware of what students can do to make teaching and learning easier or harder' (Year 10 researcher); 'Seeing other people's behaviour has helped me to think about mine' (Year 9 researcher). Students' investigations help them to tune into the thinking behind current procedures and practices in their schools, and to understand the school as an organization, particularly in appreciating its complexities and difficulties. 'They can see themselves as people who can control their own learning and can direct it because they can understand it', as one Students as Researchers coordinator remarked.

Benefits for teachers

Developing more positive relationships with students

Students as Researchers projects are rewarding for teachers in a number of ways. Teachers who have been directly involved in student research projects often express a sense of excitement. They argue that they enjoy working intensively with a smaller group of students than is usual in their teaching. They can get to know students in a different way, outside the classroom, and they often work with students they don't teach, including different age groups. They are often surprised and delighted by young people's maturity, insight and capabilities.

Teachers also come to understand students' perspectives. They 'learn about learning' from the student's standpoint and this can help new teaching approaches emerge as teachers take back to the classroom the approaches they have seen working in the context of a Students as Researchers project.

More broadly, Students as Researchers can contribute to a changing climate of staff–student relationships as teachers come to rethink their attitudes to students' capabilities. They realize that young people are 'wise' to them, that they have insight into the processes of teaching and learning and that they care about their education. They often develop greater trust, more positive attitudes and higher expectations of what groups of students can do.

These projects can help create a climate conducive to improving the conditions for teaching and learning. One example of 'how' Students as Researchers has helped raise achievement is where it leads teachers to reassess student capabilities and set them more challenging work – something that is particularly important in Years 8–9 or Year 5, where excitement about learning can flag.

The enquiry itself can contribute to teachers' continuing professional development. Some argue that the students' research can act as a valuable reminder of what they already know to be good practice. For example, as one subject teacher commented: 'It's just bringing it all back together again, reminding you of the things you actually learned during your PGCE.' Teachers comment on how powerful it can be hearing this from students. Some, however, argue that students can give valuable feedback to teachers which can help them move forward in their practice. One secondary deputy head, for example, explained how one member of staff had been at the school for twenty-five years and was 'impervious' to a lot of professional development. When Ofsted or fellow colleagues had observed him, they had acclaimed his teaching uncritically. When students observed him, they said, 'You always question to the right. And you walk up and down the aisles and the students have told us that they find that really intimidating'. The teacher later told staff that the experience of being observed by students (at his own request) and being part of the ensuing dialogue about the data collected was the most profound professional development activity he had ever experienced.

Benefits for schools

The impact on school culture and school improvement

For schools, Students as Researchers projects bring many of the benefits that have been associated with higher levels of student involvement generally. Research has suggested that student participation sets up a 'benign cycle', generating motivation, a sense of ownership, confidence and responsible attitudes and commitment, which may in turn be associated with greater engagement with learning and higher attainment (Ashworth 1995; Hannam 2003). Students as Researchers can also make specific contributions to school improvement. For instance, student enquiry can play a powerful symbolic role in the school's vision of a learning community. As one deputy head argued, 'It makes a statement about our belief that we can learn from students as much as they can learn from us'. Students as Researchers exemplifies a school's commitment to developing active, questioning students with a sense of responsibility and an enthusiasm for learning – qualities young people will require when they leave school.

To include students as part of the process of school improvement is an indication of organizational maturity and confidence, demonstrating the school's readiness to extend the boundaries of its own understanding. Student enquiry projects, especially when they are set within a broader culture of teacher enquiry, help schools become 'learning organizations' whose members can identify their own issues and priorities and therefore become self-evaluating.

Moreover, students are likely to be attracted to a school community where their views are valued: as a teacher observed, 'there is a ripple effect as word gets round that the school is one that listens to students'. Students as Researchers projects indicate a commitment to *enacting* and not merely teaching about citizenship. Finally, they often involve partnerships with outside institutions (such as universities) that can help the school be both forward- and outward-looking.

> Does the case presented here for the benefits of Students as Researchers projects resonate with your own experience and beliefs?

5. How do you start and sustain student enquiry?

The development of Students as Researchers and student enquiry requires careful planning and discussion, so that all those involved are clear about what is expected.

This section discusses:

- ensuring effective communication systems;
- how to involve students;
- choosing topics to research;
- establishing staff roles;
- matching enquiry strategies to the topic;
- resourcing and facilitating student enquiry;
- the importance of building trust;
- guiding the process;
- analysing and sharing the process and findings;
- building and developing student enquiry traditions.

Effective communication systems

Before Students as Researchers work has even begun, it is essential to develop shared understandings about lines of communication and responsibility, and about the aims, process and likely outcomes of the project. The following points need to be considered.

- Students must be assured that the research they are undertaking is real and not a cosmetic exercise, and that others will not hijack the project.
- If the enquiry extends beyond a single classroom, it is helpful if a senior manager expresses active support for the work from the beginning.
- Good systems not just for informing staff and other students, but also for involving them in the process should be established at the outset.
- It is important to consider how the research reports might relate to other student-led activities, such as the Student Council, and to relevant teacher groups such as teacher research or curriculum development groups.
- It is essential to be clear about who will act on the research outcomes.
- The relevant senior manager(s) should give a considered response to any recommendations arising from the research, except where the research project is confined to an individual classroom teacher. Students will understand if their desired course of action is not possible, provided that the reasons are clearly explained. However, failure to take the recommendations or findings of the project seriously will undermine students' trust in future Students as Researchers activities.

How to involve students

A crucial issue concerns how students come to be involved. This depends in part on the aims of the project, on the context in which teachers are working (for instance, across school structures or in a single classroom), on the kind of topics to be researched and also on the existing school culture and relationships.

Selection of students by staff

This can be a 'safe' option, especially at the start of such work, and allows the groups to be shaped as teachers would like (e.g. in terms of gender balance). However, lack of transparency about selection can make the project seem elitist, creating resentment and undermining support from other students. Staff could overlook the needs and potential contribution of the most excluded groups of students – whose views may be particularly crucial for school development.

Open recruitment

Situations where students volunteer can give the undertaking credibility and the process itself raises awareness of the initiative. However, the risk here is that those who are confident enough to volunteer may not be representative of the whole student body, and groups may not be balanced (e.g. in terms of gender).

As projects develop, staff may feel more confident about working with a wider range of students, and staff and students can work together to recruit more mixed groups. It is important to remember that involving a wide range of students in discussing school issues is not an invariably harmonious experience. However, conflicts can be a sign of democratic strength rather than weakness, representing those who have not been heard finally finding a voice and demanding recognition; as such, they are often creative and generate new insights.

If student enquiry is a cross-school initiative, questions about how the groups are to be constructed should be considered, particularly in relation to age and friendships. Older students, for instance, require less training – in secondary schools, they are likely to have some research skills already. However, they will soon leave school and won't be around to pass on their skills. Younger students often astound staff and other students by their abilities, and help ensure the project lasts, as they can continue, perhaps taking on different roles; yet they may require more training and support at particular stages. Mixed age groups can offer very positive experiences of collaboration across years and are often the only chance students have to work in this way. However, it is important to help them bond so that younger students are not intimidated, and to strike a balance between supporting younger students but still challenging older ones – for instance, by asking older students to act as mentors to younger ones.

Too many students in a research group may mean it becomes less focused and organized, unless those involved are used to working with each other – as in a case where a teacher works with a whole class. Too few may create too heavy a workload for those involved. An average of six to eight students per team has enabled successful collaboration in research projects. However, each team could be part of a larger enterprise, provided each can be resourced and supported properly.

Choosing topics to research

Students as Researchers groups may be brought together to discuss existing issues that the school, or an individual teacher working within their classroom, has decided to address through student research. Alternatively, students may join a research group out of a general interest in investigation, deciding the precise topics later.

A key debate here concerns who decides what to research. Will the boundaries be set in advance? Where is there a real chance of change? Equally, is there a culture of silence in the school that results in students censoring themselves about important issues? What are the limits, and are these clear to all parties? Where staff decide on the issues for enquiry (for instance, according to the school development agenda or a teacher's particular interest), information is likely to be useful and so lead to change. However, students may lack involvement and commitment; and it cuts off the possibility that students may raise important but overlooked issues. Where student researchers themselves choose the topics, they are likely to be motivated to see it through. However, it is important that staff understand and support the topics, and that other students feel that they represent their own views and concerns. Selection of topics through a system of voting by all relevant students can help develop commitment to the initiative and give student researchers a clear responsibility to act on behalf of others – although it may also mean that populist options win out.

In practice, there is often consensus between all parties over what issues are important and a combination approach (drawing on elements of all three methods of choosing topics) can work well. If students' concerns prove to be out of step with teacher or management priorities, this itself gives valuable information about the school community.

Establishing staff roles

Teachers should be available to support the Students as Researchers group – their contribution is often crucial to the success and smooth running of the process. However, their role may be quite different to the role they play in formal class teaching, and both sides need to be clear about this and adjust to it. The kinds of role staff may play include: helping to organize, encourage, prompt or coordinate; administrating; acting as advocates and go-betweens with other staff and other adults; helping with the sequencing and structure of the work; promoting good group dynamics; and sharing wider knowledge about the school to put things into perspective. And, importantly, it also involves teachers learning to step back and allow students to get on with the work. Increasingly, administrative staff and other support staff are working alongside students, especially younger ones, to support them in this process.

It is important to keep support and administrative staff fully informed about the work, especially if they are likely to be asked to help with booking rooms, arranging photocopying or passing on messages about meetings.

Access to external support in the form of mentoring, critical friends, sharing ideas at conferences and workshops or visiting other schools can help teachers maintain energy. Many teachers have begun Students as Researchers work whilst studying for an MA or educational diploma.

Matching enquiry strategies to the topic

When research topics have been identified, students and teachers need to find appropriate ways of finding answers. Students tend to assume that conventional research instruments such as surveys and question-naires are the best approach, rather than using more in-depth or creative qualitative approaches. Students may therefore need to be introduced to alternatives. A useful way of thinking about the work might be to consider what insights student research might provide that professional forms of enquiry miss. Students as Researchers work may be seen as a way of making the 'unofficial' knowledge about teaching and learning that circulates between students more widely available and understood. Accessing such knowledge may require innovative approaches. For instance, one research project invited Year 7 students to make collages about their feelings about being new to the school, which they then talked about in discussions. Another accessible way of getting data is through photographs; for example, students have taken photos around the school of places where they feel safe or unsafe (MacBeath *et al.* 2003).

One dilemma concerns what happens if the quality of students' work seems weak – for instance, if questionnaires or surveys are badly worded or poorly thought out. Teachers not involved might dismiss the research as having little value because they feel it is based on inadequate instruments. On the other hand, if the teachers supporting the Students as Researchers group correct and improve the work too much, the researchers may feel that the project is no longer 'theirs'. If the process appears to be a highly specialized and 'academic' activity, it may alienate some young people within the school and make them less willing to contribute, either as respondents or as researchers. Solutions to such dilemmas include the careful piloting of research instruments and good communication about the nature of the work to those who may be asked to respond to it.

Resourcing and facilitating student enquiry

Finding time to carry out the enquiry is always a difficult issue. Meeting at lunchtime is a common option, although it means that students' enthusiasm is crucial. In some schools, student enquiry is a timetabled extra-curricular option, or part of Citizenship Education. Students are often willing to come in during staff INSET or CPD days in order to present their findings or work-in-progress and tackle more substantial aspects of the research. Inductions for new student researchers in secondary schools can take place after the exams in the summer term when there is often more flexibility in the timetable. If students are to be involved in observing teaching and learning outside their own classroom or interviewing young people in other classes or schools, they will need to be allowed to do so during lesson time – which in turn means that other staff need to be aware and supportive of the projects, as do the parents of those involved.

Time is also a common concern for teachers, and schools' responsiveness and sensitivity to this issue is crucial. For example, one secondary school that was committed to supporting and developing student voice work built into its timetable one shared non-contact period a fortnight for the three participating staff.

Students as Researchers projects are not expensive to run, but they cannot be done for nothing. Support and understanding from senior managers and governors is therefore important. Possible requirements include meeting space; providing food and drink during meetings (to treat students as other adults would be treated in a similar situation); cover for teachers to accompany students to conferences; travel; stationery and access to photocopying and clerical support, for instance, in notifying students of meetings. More substantial costs might be incurred if, for instance, a teacher is given a responsibility point to coordinate the work, or for training. Giving students a budget that is under their control is a powerful indicator of how far the school genuinely desires to share responsibility and power in decision-making.

The importance of building trust

Students as Researchers projects also need to create a space in which students and staff can come together in a different way and work together in a partnership. Early gatherings of the student researchers and the teacher or teachers working with them are important in establishing the parameters of the research and modelling new ways of working. Some starting points that have been found useful have included considering what different people (students, teachers, senior managers, outsiders) might each contribute to the process; sharing hopes, fears and expectations of the research; and working out ground rules that will guide the conduct of the research. For instance, in one school, students and teachers came up with the acronym 'SHORT' to describe their values: S, sensitive; H, honest; O, open; R, respect; T, trust.

Guiding the process

Student researchers need to be given the chance to acquire research skills and the social skills of listening, responding and negotiating that will enable them to contribute to – and ultimately take charge of – the research. Some schools draw on internal expertise to help with research methods, such as social science teachers or colleagues with research experience. In other cases, schools have been able to involve external figures who arrange or offer training and provide ongoing support for the student groups. Trainers can reinforce the work of teachers in supporting students but in addition, they may offer encouragement by setting the students' work in a wider context. They may help extend students' understanding of the subtleties of research and offer training in more participatory research techniques – such as drawing, role-play, photography, mapping/ timelines, group work – rather than, or as well as, the established ones such as surveys, questionnaires and interviews, to which students often turn initially. Finally, they may act as a first 'audience' for the findings – someone to whom students can present what they have done, who acts as a sounding board for their thinking. Students are often motivated by developing relationships with an outsider whose opinion they respect and value. Whilst outside trainers can involve costs, some schools have formed consortia to supply training at less cost to individual schools.

In some cases, students who already possess certain key skills, knowledge and experience may consistently put themselves forward (or be put forward by other group members) to take on leadership positions. Although they may have good intentions, such practices may ultimately undermine other students' confidence, perpetuate familiar hierarchies in terms of who takes on what roles and mean that the group fails to be representative of the wider student body. Time and care can be given early on to considering what skills the group collectively possesses and how these might be passed on – for instance, by less confident students shadowing others for a limited period of time and then taking over those roles.

Analysing and sharing the process and findings

Although data gathering – running discussion groups, observing lessons or interviewing – often seems the most exciting and motivating part of the research, sufficient time must be left for making sense of it. A large quantity of data is often gathered, even from a few interviews. Analysing data might follow a number of steps:

- keeping a record of what information was gathered and how;
- noting hitches experienced along the way;
- breaking it down to analyse it;
- drawing conclusions and checking back to see if the data support them;
- producing a report or record of the work;
- deciding how formal the report will be depending on the context of the work and its likely audience, such as other students, parents, staff or governors.

Communicating before, during and after the process is crucial and involves both informing and the process of dialogue. Informing involves letting people know what is planned and explaining to those who may be involved in or affected by the research why their time is needed and what the outcome of the research might be. Dialogue, on the other hand, involves providing opportunities for others to discuss the research and to influence it, helping others feel they have a stake in what is being done and sharing work in progress. Whilst information is important, dialogue may be more significant in bringing about widespread positive outcomes and significant 'cultural' change.

Everyone involved in the research should receive clear feedback. This serves to value what the student researchers have done as well as what others may have contributed. Students often find imaginative means of sharing findings. For instance, one group of sixth formers put selected quotations from their research report on the college screensaver to encourage people to read the whole report that was on the college intranet. Other students have used the school's radio or television broadcasting facilities to reach a wide audience. Word of mouth is also very powerful – many teachers become interested by seeing what the students have been achieving through their involvement and in hearing from them.

Students work extremely hard at their research and it is often the possibility of affecting practice that motivates them. It is essential that the relevant staff provide a thoughtful response to it, as we noted above. This does not, of course, always mean that recommendations are able to be implemented; it does always mean that student enquiry work is appropriately honoured. Staff should recognize and celebrate what has been achieved, for instance through individual letters to those involved, public congratulations at events such as parents' and awards evenings or credit for youth awards schemes. Where action is taken as a consequence of the research, it is worth highlighting this to students.

Dialogue also means recognizing that the results are open to interpretation and are not definitive. Teachers may disagree with students' views as expressed in their reports, although they offer valuable insight into students' concerns that need to be addressed. In some schools, staff training time has been given over to discussing the students' reports. This has worked particularly well when students are present to explain their research questions and methods and to respond in more detail to teachers' queries.

Engaging with others might also go beyond the individual school. Learning with and from other schools, both locally and nationally (even internationally), is increasingly recognized as important for school improvement.

There may be divergences of opinion over whether it is the actual outcomes of the report – the recommendations – that matter, or the process that led to it. On the one hand, students may have high expectations of the impact of the actual report and seek definite responses to it. Parents or governors may query the value of the work unless they can see concrete outcomes. For many teachers, however, it may be the process that matters most. Teachers are often very impressed to see students conducting themselves responsibly and becoming more active in their approach to learning and school improvement. They are often pleased and surprised at the amount of common ground between them. This 'culture change' in relationships and perceptions might seem more important than the research findings or, indeed, may not be adequately captured by a report. Thus, it is important to bear in mind the less immediately obvious marks of change in the culture of the school. These might include, for instance, teachers within individual classrooms feeling more confident about handing over responsibility to students, and more open to students suggesting alternative ways of approaching their learning.

There is no doubt that senior staff and heads have to include amongst their number one or more 'champions' of the work. Some staff and parents may be concerned that participation projects distract students from their assessed schoolwork. In these cases it is vital that senior staff are prepared to defend the personal and academic value of such work and present evidence of its positive outcomes. They need also to act as champions of students. They should believe not only that young people are capable of working in these ways, but also that it is a good thing to encourage them to do so, and they should be able to recognize and respect what they achieve.

Building and developing student enquiry traditions

As time goes by, it is worth considering how to build capacity and help Students as Researchers projects become a more established feature of how the school operates. Existing student researchers may want to repeat the experience or take on new roles – such as monitoring changes as a result of previous research recommendations, helping to involve and train new students or acting as 'consultants' or advisors to new groups. Make sure that information about the projects is part of the induction of incoming staff so that they become aware of the research traditions of the school as far as possible, and enthuse other staff.

Are there any further queries and questions that remain having read the advice given here about how to develop the practice of Students as Researchers activities?

6. What dilemmas and issues are posed by the development of Students as Researchers activities?

The development of Students as Researchers activities represents a significant shift of practice for many practitioners, and it is important to think through the concerns that they may have. It is important as well to be aware of the limitations of student enquiry. This section includes:

- practitioner concerns: whose voices, whose purposes?
- the limitations of student enquiry and the possible pitfalls.

Practitioner concerns: whose voices, whose purposes?

When encouraging student enquiry, particularly into issues of teaching and learning, it is important to be sensitive to the genuine anxiety felt by teachers who have not experienced this way of working before. Teachers may be sceptical about young people's knowledge, intentions or capabilities. They may feel that children are not competent to offer comments on their work, that they may not keep confidentiality or that it gives a platform to the 'wrong' students. Some teachers have felt that students do not fully understand the complexities of the context or the system in which they operate. However negative outcomes are less likely where students are supported in their work and enabled to understand the broader context of their activities, and where issues of values and ethics are addressed early on and returned to throughout the process.

Student enquiry is unlikely to succeed unless teachers too are continuing learners – involved in seeking new ideas, analysing results, being reflective, trying out new practices and working with others. The opportunities that a school provides for staff to get involved in action research and other forms of professional enquiry are therefore crucial – as has been discussed elsewhere in this book.

The limitations of student enquiry and the possible pitfalls

It is important to be reflective and self-aware about the limitations of student enquiry. For instance, we should recognize that consultation and participation tend to require particular skills or dispositions, such as being able to articulate viewpoints in an 'acceptable' form, and a conciliatory or positive attitude towards school and teachers. Issues of social class within our society are as germane to student enquiry as any other aspect of schooling (Arnot *et al.* 2001). As Elena Silva so eloquently urges: 'We must recognize that the school's embossed invitation to participate looks unfamiliar, unattractive, or out of reach to many students, especially those in most need of serious changes in their school' (Silva 2001, p. 98). Whilst most schools recognize the risks of creating new elites within the student body they are often less aware of the very real danger of missing out on the voices of those who are quiet, silenced or even angry (see, for example, Bragg 2001; Cruddas 2001; Mitra 2001; Silva 2001) – yet whose viewpoints are nonetheless crucial for genuine school improvement. So much is demanded of teachers and students we find it difficult to create the space and nurture the dispositions to be open and attentive over time and in time:

The pressures of needing rapid results may lead us to listen most readily to voices that make immediate sense. ... (We need) to take our time with the anomalous (and) allow what doesn't fit or produces unexpected reactions in us to disrupt our assumptions and habitual ways of working (since) it is from these that we may, in the end, learn most.

(Bragg 2001, p. 72)

We should be thoughtful about the nature of the student 'voice' and the claims we make about its authenticity. We also need to ask sharp questions about whose purposes are being served by the recent upsurge of interest in and commitment to consulting young people. Both Ofsted and the DfES now have substantial sophisticated arrangements for listening to the views of students and we now have a Children's Commissioner for Wales who is taking very seriously the importance of listening and responding to young people in his country. The world is seldom all for or all against developments such as those we have been advocating in this chapter and it may well be we need more sophisticated analyses of these different perspectives (Bragg 2003; Fielding 2001c). Nonetheless, we need to scrutinize honestly the evidence of emerging work in the field for the claimed creativity and beneficence that the difference in standpoint between young people and adults is supposed to produce. Are students simply ventriloquizing predictable teacher-approved ideas, or are they bringing insights that are genuinely fresh and even challenging to those who are listening?

At the very practical day-to-day level, a number of teachers have found our framework for 'Evaluating the conditions for student voice' (Fielding 2001a and c) helpful, not only for evaluating student voice practices within their own schools, but also for prompting thought about how things might be developed in sustainable and creative ways.

Within your own context would there be any other issues posed by the development of Students as Researchers? If there are, how might you go about addressing them?

Evaluating the conditions for student voice

Speaking	• <u>Who</u> is allowed to speak? • <u>To whom</u> are they allowed to speak? • <u>What</u> are they allowed to speak about?
Listening	• <u>Who</u> is listening? • <u>Why</u> are they listening? • <u>How</u> are they listening?
Skills	• Are the skills of dialogue <u>encouraged and supported</u> through training or other appropriate means? • Are those skills understood, developed and practiced within the <u>context of democratic values and dispositions</u>?
Attitudes & dispositions	• How do those involved <u>regard each other</u>? • To what degree are the <u>principle of equal value</u> and the <u>dispositions of care</u> felt reciprocally and demonstrated through the reality of daily encounter?
Systems	• <u>How often</u> does dialogue and encounter in which student voice is centrally important occur? • How do the systems enshrining the value and necessity of student voice mesh with or <u>relate to other organizational arrangements</u> (particularly those involving adults)?
Organizational culture	• Do the <u>cultural norms and values</u> of the school proclaim the centrality of student voice within the context of education as a shared responsibility and shared achievement? • Do the <u>practices, traditions and routine daily encounters</u> demonstrate values supportive of student voice?
Spaces & the making of meaning	• <u>Where</u> are the public spaces (physical and metaphorical) in which these encounters might take place? • Who <u>controls</u> them? • What <u>values</u> shape their being and their use?
Action	• What <u>action</u> is taken? • Who feels <u>responsible</u>? • <u>What happens</u> if aspirations and good intentions are not realized?
The future	• Do we need <u>new structures</u>? • Do we need <u>new ways of relating to each other</u>?

Endpiece

The student enquiry projects discussed here have proved to be a rewarding and positive experience both for young people and for teachers and other school staff. For students, the research projects offer the chance to explore new and different identities as researchers. They represent a bridge between school and the adult or external world, in terms of the activities they involve and the dispositions and skills they develop – such as working independently and in teams, across hierarchies of age and status. Our evidence shows how motivating students find this – one student described it as 'that extra niche that I needed in order to keep me interested in my studies and motivate me to come to school'. In the process, young people acquire attitudes and skills that help them become lifelong learners, or as one deputy head put it, they become 'people who can control their own learning and can direct it because they can understand it'.

In addition, Students as Researchers activities enable students to contribute to the development of the whole school. Students have conducted relevant enquiries that have yielded important insights into teaching and learning from a student perspective – or have provided, as one head described it, 'the consumer insight, which we don't normally get'. Talk of 'consumer rights' within education often refers only to parents, not to the young people who have most experience of contemporary schooling. Students as Researchers represents a significant shift in how students are perceived. They are invited to form constructive partnerships with staff, where they play an active role in reflecting on the purposes and workings of school and in formulating ideas for improvement. Thus students comment that, 'It was an equal thing ... It wasn't like the teacher was telling us what to do', and teachers say, 'It's not about students picking holes in teachers, it's about achieving together'.

The process has led to improved relationships between staff and students. Teachers come to revalue students' capabilities in the process; as one teacher commented, 'it puts me back in touch with the inspirational side of [teaching], because their insights into their lives in school always exceed my expectations'.

It allows schools as institutions to reflect on teaching and learning processes. As one head argued, 'When you want to actually start making a difference closer to the classroom then the students' perception of what's going on becomes quite important'. As traditions of student enquiry grow and develop, new kinds of structures and spaces are emerging in schools, which belong neither to staff only (e.g. staff meetings) nor to students (student council meetings), but to both as co-facilitators of change. Already, instances where students run workshops on INSET days or join with teachers as equal members of an enquiry team or an evaluation group looking at new curriculum provision, have the capacity to shift school cultures and structures in ways that redefine the boundaries of traditional roles of 'teachers' and 'students'. At its best and in the right circumstances, Students as Researchers is a 'boundary practice', where not only the tasks and conditions of learning have changed, but where the traditional roles and relations between teachers and students become more fluid and open to renegotiation. This is not about collaboration; rather it is about collegiality, a 'radical collegiality' (Fielding 1999) in which it is, on occasions, possible for teachers to learn from students, for students to teach teachers, and for both to understand in their hearts and in their actions that learning is at once joyful and terrifying, unpredictable and demanding of our patience and trust in each other. Above all, significant learning is not possible unless it is connected to a deeper narrative in which we struggle to understand who we are and who we wish to become together. This requires not only that we change our understanding of what it is to be a teacher, what it is to be a student. It also requires that schools transcend the belligerent and deeply corrosive imperatives of schools as high-performance learning organizations and instead become person-centred learning communities (Fielding 2000a and b). There are some grounds for thinking that, under certain conditions and with the inspiration of particular teachers and particular schools, initiatives like Students as Researchers might contribute towards the beginnings of such as process. It is long overdue. More depends on it than we think: it deserves our support.

This chapter draws on material previously published by Michael Fielding and Sara Bragg (2003) as *Students as Researchers: Making a Difference*, Cambridge: Pearson's Publishing. Much of the research reported in this book was undertaken for a project entitled 'Consulting Pupils about Teaching and Learning (2000–2003)' funded by the Economic and Social Research Council's Teaching and Learning Research Programme. We are grateful for the support, participation and encouragement of all the schools, students and teachers involved in the project, and also to the many who contributed indirectly.

References

Alderson, P. and Arnold, S. (1999) 'Civil Rights in Schools' ESRC Children 5 16 Programme Briefing no. 1.

Arnot, M., Reay, D., Flutter, J. and Wang, B. (2001) 'Pupil consultation and the social conditions of learning: race, class and gender identities and participation as learners: how pupils can help teachers improve the social conditions of learning', paper presented at the Annual Meeting of the American Educational Research Association, Seattle.

Ashworth, L. (1995) *Children's Voices in School Matters*, London: Advisory Centre for Education.

Bragg, S. (2001) 'Taking a joke: learning from voices we don't want to hear', *Forum* 43(2): 70–3.

Bragg, S. (2003) 'Student voice and governmentality: the production of enterprising subjects', paper presented at the Annual conference of the British Educational Research Association, Edinburgh.

Crane, B. (2001) 'Revolutionising school-based research', *Forum* 43(2): 54–5.

Cruddas, L. (2001) 'Rehearsing for reality: young women's voices and agendas for change', *Forum* 43(2): 62–6.

Fielding, M. (1998) 'Students as researchers: from data source to significant voice', paper presented at the International Congress for School Effectiveness and School Improvement, University of Manchester, January.

Fielding, M. (1999) 'Radical collegiality: affirming teaching as an inclusive professional practice', *Australian Educational Researcher* 26(2), August: 1–34.

Fielding, M. (2000a) 'The Person Centred School', *Forum* 42(2): 51–4.

Fielding, M. (2000b) 'Community, philosophy and education policy: against effectiveness ideology and the immiseration of contemporary schooling', *Journal of Educational Policy* 15(4): 397–415.

Fielding, M. (2001a) 'Target setting, policy pathology and student perspectives: learning to labour in new times', in M. Fielding (ed.) *Taking Education Really Seriously: Four Years Hard Labour*, London: Routledge Falmer pp. 143–54.

Fielding, M. (2001b) 'Students as radical agents of change', *Journal of Educational Change* 2(3): 123–41.

Fielding, M. (2001c) 'Beyond the rhetoric of student voice: new departures or new constraints in the transformation of 21st century schooling?', *Forum* 43(2): 100–10.

Fielding, M. (2004) 'Transformative approaches to student voice:

theoretical underpinnings, recalcitrant realities', *British Educational Research Journal* 30(2): 295–311.

Fielding, M. and Bragg, S. (2003) *Students as Researchers: Making a Difference*, Cambridge: Pearson Publishing Group.

Fielding, M. and Prieto, M. (2000) 'Investiganio con estudiantes: una experiencia de practica democratica', *Paideia* 28: 105–28.

Hannam, D. H. (2003) 'Participation and achievement: examples of research that demonstrate associations or connections between student participation and learning, or other outcomes that support it', unpublished Literature review commissioned by DfES and Cambridge University.

Hannam, D. H. (2004) *Involving young people in identifying ways of gathering their views on the curriculum*, London: QCA.

Harding, C. (2001) '"Students as researchers" is as important as the national curriculum', *Forum* 43(2): 56–7.

Holdsworth, R. (2000a) 'Taking young people seriously means giving them serious things to do', in J. Mason and M. Wilkinson, (eds) *Taking Children Seriously*, Sydney, Australia: University of Western Sydney.

Holdsworth, R. (2000b) 'Schools that create real roles of value for young people', *Prospects* 30(3), September: 349–62.

Kirby, P. (1999) *Involving Young Researchers: how to enable young people to design and conduct research*, York: Joseph Rowntree Foundation.

Kirby, P. (2001) 'Participatory research in schools', *Forum* 43(2): 74–7.

Levin, B. (1998) 'The educational requirement for democracy', *Curriculum Inquiry* 28(1): 57–79.

Levin, B. (2000a) 'Putting students at the centre of educational reform', *Journal of Educational Change* 1(2): 155–72.

Levin, B. (2000b) 'Democracy and schools', *Education Canada* 40(3): 4–7.

Lincoln, Y. (1995) 'In search of students' voices', *Theory into Practice* 34(2), Spring: 88–93.

MacBeath, J., Rudduck, J., Demetriou, H. and Myers, K. (2003) *Consulting Pupils: A Toolkit for Teachers*, Cambridge: Pearson Publishing Group.

Mitra, D. (2001) 'Opening the floodgates: giving students a voice in school reform', *Forum* 43(2): 91–4.

Oldfather, P. (1995) 'Songs "Come Back Most to Them": students' experiences as researchers', *Theory into Practice* 34(2), Spring: 131–7.

Prieto, M. (2001) 'Students as agents of democratic renewal in Chile', *Forum* 43(2): 87–90.

Raymond, L. (2001) 'Student involvement in school improvement: from data source to significant voice', *Forum* 43(2): 58–61.

Silva, E. (2001) '"Squeaky wheels and flat tires": a case study of students as reform participants', *Forum* 43(2): 95–9.

Steinberg, S. and Kincheloe, J. (1998) (eds) *Students as Researchers*, London: Falmer.

Wetherill, L. (1998) 'The "Students as Researchers" Project at Sharnbrook Upper School and Community College', *Improving Schools* 1(2): 52–3.

Worrall, N., Wheeler, N., Ward, A. and James, M. (1999) '"Students as researchers" at Queen Elizabeth's Girls' School', University of Cambridge School of Education Newsletter No. 5 pp. 3–5.

Wyse, D. (2001) 'Felt tip pens and school councils: children's participation rights in four English schools', *Children and Society* 15: 209–18.

Summary and conclusion

Julie Temperley and Hilary Street

Throughout the book a summary of the main points discussed has been given on a chapter-by-chapter basis. What this summary seeks to do is to highlight the key learning points that have been developed throughout the book and provide an overview of the importance and relevance of collaborative enquiry for practitioners in education.

Defining 'collaborative enquiry'

This book has explored a definition of collaborative enquiry by identifying and discussing the characteristics of collaborative enquiry and the principles that underpin it. In broad terms, collaborative enquiry is a particular form of school-based research. It involves practitioners collaborating together to enquire into an aspect of practice with the specific intention of developing their own classroom practice and sharing their findings with other colleagues both within and beyond their own context. Investigating what research knowledge already exists on their chosen theme is an integral part of the process.

In discussing definitions of collaborative enquiry we considered its relationship as a concept to the development of informed professionalism and of teaching as a research and evidence informed profession.

The importance of collaborative enquiry at this time for the education system in general and schools in particular

We believe that collaborative enquiry is an essential process for all schools to engage in at this time for three reasons: the implications of the external context in which schools operate; its usefulness as a change management strategy; and the importance of the 'transformation agenda'.

We have discussed the view that school improvement is moving into a third phase, that of 'authentic' school improvement, and collaborative enquiry is a central part of that. Externally driven change and top-down national strategies are no longer sufficient to meet the demands made on schools in the twenty-first century. Schools have to be more proactive in finding their own responses to those challenges and collaborative enquiry is one strategy schools can use to increase the capacity of their practitioners to respond positively and productively to the challenges and changes. The demands of the 'knowledge society' require practitioners in schools to develop their own professional expertise and professional capacity to be able to make sense of their changing context and to continue to respond to the challenge of continual development and growth, both for themselves and their pupils. Collaborative enquiry with its clear focus on the practice of learning and teaching in individual classrooms has the potential to be an effective professional development strategy for practitioners, which, because it is generated by the practitioners themselves in the light of their own practice, is more likely to impact directly on their classrooms.

The process of collaborative enquiry requires practitioners to investigate the knowledge and research base which already exists and relate that to their own current knowledge and practice. This was illustrated in the 'Three circles of knowledge' diagram. In this way collaborative enquiry links directly to the development of 'informed professionalism' on the part of all practitioners.

Collaborative enquiry also has implications for the changing view of continuing professional development (CPD). Our understanding of effective CPD processes and opportunities, particularly with reference to those that have an impact on pupil learning, has developed substantially, with a move away from one-off off-site courses to more school-based development that is directly linked to classroom practice with the intention of impacting both on teacher learning and pupil learning. Collaborative enquiry is an effective CPD strategy as it enables practitioners to both build on their own knowledge and use existing knowledge and research to identify appropriate interventions for their particular context. In addition, it enables the principles of effective learning, which apply to both practitioners and pupils, to inform the design of the enquiry process so the preferred ways of learning of the practitioners involved can be accommodated. It also encourages a 'contructivist' view of learning since enquiries are designed to be social processes where colleagues work together on new and existing knowledge to inform their practice.

Schools in the UK and elsewhere are under increasing pressure to 'transform' themselves to be 'fit for purpose' for the twenty-first century. The transformation agenda necessitates leaders in schools developing the social, intellectual and organizational capital within their organizations to enable that transformation to take place. Collaborative enquiry is a way of working that can impact on all three. One outcome from the development of social, intellectual and organizational capital is the increase in 'distributed leadership' within an organization. This happens because the process of collaborative enquiry involves more members of the school community in leadership roles and because the leadership of an enquiry does not have to be undertaken by someone who already has a formal leadership role in the school, though sometimes that may be the case.

Collaborative enquiry is an important strategy because it makes a difference to practice. It is non-hierarchical in nature and an inclusive activity, driven by practitioners and therefore more likely to be relevant to the perceived needs of those involved and grounded in classroom practice.

The key characteristics and elements of effective collaborative enquiry

We believe collaborative enquiry takes shape in different ways depending on the particular context. This is why it has the potential to be such an effective learning strategy. However there are some key characteristics and some key activities that seem to be present in most examples of effective collaborative enquiry. They include the importance of taking the current school context as the starting point and problematizing the day-to-day work. This means looking with fresh eyes at what is currently happening in classrooms and not making assumptions about what is going on, but questioning what is taken for granted. Although the school context is the starting point, practitioners actively seek out information from elsewhere about existing relevant research and practice in order to inform their own thinking. This means they are engaging in a process of investigation that is rigorous, disciplined and relevant to their context. An important part of the enquiry process is about gathering information (qualitative and quantitative data) about what is currently happening in the school that relates to the chosen focus. This requires practitioners to develop their skills of data gathering and analysis. The purpose of the data gathering is understood by all involved to be an essential part of the process and is also managed by those involved. This is important because the 'ownership' of the data rests with the practitioners and the data is seen as a useful tool to support the enquiry process rather than as something that is potentially overtly and publicly critical of individual practice.

The process of collaborative enquiry and the outcomes of the enquiry itself actually create new knowledge, hence the process of knowledge creation is an important characteristic of collaborative enquiry. An essential characteristic of collaborative enquiry is the ability and commitment to represent the findings both during and at the end of the enquiry in such a way that they can be accessed and understood by other practitioners. Finally where collaborative enquiry is taking place effectively there will be an 'enabling' context in place because the leadership in the school will have been proactive in ensuring that working practices and processes support rather than hinder collaboration between practitioners.

The case studies in Chapter 3 illustrated the following characteristics and outcomes of collaborative enquiry:

- a choice of focus and strategies that were both 'fit for purpose' in each school or network context;
- a willingness to adapt and be flexible in different circumstances and contexts;
- a balance between content and process; both are valuable learning opportunities;
- the process in all of the examples generated trust and risk-taking;
- it is a motivating experience for both practitioners and pupils;
- the process creates the support and need for distributed leadership;
- in all cases collaborative enquiry was action orientated and designed to impact on practitioner and pupil learning;
- problem-solving was a central part of the process;
- the process of collaborative enquiry contributed to the building of a sense of community in the schools described;
- there was an impact on the nature of the conversations and relationships between the enquirers; this also included pupils;
- the process of collaborative enquiry brings discipline to innovation and implementation strategies and supports a rigour of approach and analysis;
- collaborative enquiry was fun for the participants!

Collaborative enquiry impacts on staff, pupils and the school

We believe that collaborative enquiry makes a difference to practice, and examples of that are included in Chapter 3 and elsewhere in this book. Collaborative enquiry also impacts on the organization of a school and its working practices. We have given examples of the sorts of 'facilitative conditions' which school leaders need to develop to support collaborative enquiry and shown its contribution to capacity building, the development of a learning community and the development of distributed leadership in schools. Collaborative enquiry has a democratizing impact on the ways in which members of the school community relate to each other, and this extends to students. We have shown how the role of Students as Researchers is a logical extension of the process of collaborative enquiry. It has the potential to be an inclusive activity involving teachers, pupils, support staff and other members of the school community as appropriate.

Collaborative enquiry within and between schools

Collaborative enquiry can happen both within and between schools and examples of both types of activity were discussed. An important point of principle for the development of collaborative enquiry is that it should transcend organizational boundaries.

Collaborative enquiry has significant implications for school leaders

The implications of collaborative enquiry for leadership in schools were discussed, in particular the responsibility on leaders to create enabling conditions for practitioners to engage in enquiry. In addition, collaborative enquiry has an impact on leadership at all levels in schools and leads to more distributed leadership. The sorts of processes and practices that leaders can develop include: identifying a member of staff to support and coordinate collaborative enquiry; developing effective communication systems to support enquiry; putting in place professional development opportunities so that staff can acquire and practise the necessary skills; and leaders themselves modelling enquiry processes.

We therefore believe that schools who develop collaborative enquiry as a 'metabolic' taken-for-granted way of working will be open, warm and welcoming organizations. Both staff, pupils and students will feel pleased to belong to the organization and will feel valued. High standards of professional practice will be the norm, and staff will be pleased to be working within the culture of high expectations. Pupils and students will be responding to that culture and will be striving to achieve their best and be the 'best that they can be'. They will feel valued and respected. Questioning and professional dialogue will be the norm.

Such schools will be wonderful places to live and learn in at whatever age and in whatever role!

INDEX

A 'f' after a page number indicates inclusion of a figure; a 't' indicates inclusion of a table

Lightning Source UK Ltd.
Milton Keynes UK
13 October 2010

161179UK00001B/65/P